"Renee Brooks Catacalos has been, and continues to be, a tireless advocate for the local food traditions of the Chesapeake Bay region. She is also a brilliant writer with a razor-sharp focus and the ability to bring to life disparate aspects of the Chesapeake, including the simple joys of home-cooked local food. This book is a welcome addition to the body of work on our magnificent Bay."—JOHN SHIELDS, Gertrude's Restaurant

"After many years of walking the walk and sharing her passion for local and sustainable food practices in various outlets, Renee Catacalos brings all of this knowledge together in one beautiful package. *The Chesapeake Table* is a must-have resource, complete with delicious recipes, showing how eating locally and sustainably is possible."—CARLA HALL, co-host of *The Chew*

"A delectable love poem to locally grown food and the people who produce it, Renee Brooks Catacalos's book makes a compelling argument for strengthening the local economy and community health by eating primarily what's grown in the Chesapeake Bay foodshed. Buy this book and digest its message that 'all our daily choices count.'"
—MARGARET MORGAN-HUBBARD, ECO City Farms

"Renee Catacalos has done a great service to the cause of local foodways in the mid-Atlantic by writing this book, a thorough, informative, and wide-ranging look at how we eat now—and how, with more support, more food hubs, and continued awareness of the ecological and social issues that affect our ever-widening food stream, we might eat in the future."
—TODD KLIMAN, author of *The Perfect Chef*

"Renee Catacalos has long been a champion of the edible resources and character of the Chesapeake watershed. Her book beautifully ties cultural, historical, and natural resources into a poetic volume that ennobles the people of the greater Chesapeake, giving an appreciation for the sustainable and local in one of America's most ancient and proud foodscapes."
—MICHAEL TWITTY, author of *The Cooking Gene: A Journey through African American Culinary History in the Old South*

"There is so much to admire and discover in Renee Catacalos's quest for the best local foods and small-scale producers in the Chesapeake foodshed. She is *the* Chesapeake locavore food maven who informs your food choices to sustain the Chesapeake."
—BERNADINE PRINCE, cofounder of FRESH

D1232292

"From produce to poultry to policy, *The Chesapeake Table* takes you on a thoroughly delicious and instructive journey through one of America's greatest and most diverse foodsheds. Fact-packed and certified to satisfy, this book has everything you'll ever need to eat local and to eat like a local."
—MARK WINNE, author of *Stand Together or Starve Alone: Unity and Chaos in the U.S. Food Movement*

"Reading this book was an absolute delight. Renee Brooks Catacalos shows not only that eating local is possible but that it is pleasurable, too, as you go foraging locally to savor the 'tastes of the region.' Read it and then seek and find local food."—DAVID KLINE, editor of *Farming Magazine*

"*The Chesapeake Table* is a delightful guide full of vital tips for those committed to cherishing and conserving the local bounty of our prized mid-Atlantic region. Renee Catacalos reveals a substantial understanding of heritage and politics, and she advocates from the perspective only a true local could offer to her readers."—TODD and ELLEN KASSOFF GRAY, Equinox Restaurant

"With her deep roots and knowledge, there is no better guide to our evolving food system than Renee Catacalos, who weaves together history, policy, and inspiring stories to create the new bible for how every person makes a difference in growing a vibrant, inclusive, and equitable food system for all."
—TANYA DENCKLA COBB, author of *Reclaiming Our Food: How the Grassroots Food Movement Is Changing the Way We Eat*

"Fascinating and delectable. If you live in the mid-Atlantic—and you eat—then read this wonderful book."
—FORREST PRITCHARD, author of *Gaining Ground: A Story of Farmers' Markets, Local Food, and Saving the Family Farm*

"*The Chesapeake Table* is a wonderful resource of history, personal stories, and actionable information on how communities live in better harmony with their food systems and one another. Catacalos makes an invaluable contribution to the robust local food discourse while placing an important spotlight on the Chesapeake foodshed."
—REV. DR. HEBER BROWN III, Black Church Food Security Network, Pleasant Hope Baptist Church

The Chesapeake Table

The Chesapeake Table

Your Guide to Eating Local

RENEE BROOKS CATACALOS

Johns Hopkins University Press
Baltimore

Johns Hopkins University Press
2715 North Charles Street
Baltimore, Maryland 21218-4363
www.press.jhu.edu

Library of Congress Cataloging-in-Publication Data
Names: Catacalos, Renee Brooks, 1963–, author.
Title: The Chesapeake Table : your guide to eating local / Renee Brooks Catacalos.
Description: Baltimore : Johns Hopkins University Press, 2018. |
Includes bibliographical references and index.
Identifiers: LCCN 2018007458 | ISBN 9781421426891 (pbk. : alk. paper) |
ISBN 1421426897 (pbk. : alk. paper) | ISBN 9781421426907 (electronic) |
ISBN 1421426900 (electronic)
Subjects: LCSH: Local foods—Chesapeake Bay Region (Md. and Va.) |
Food industry and trade—Chesapeake Bay Region (Md. and Va.)
Classification: LCC TX360.U62 M385 2018 | DDC 641.3009755/18—dc23
LC record available at https://lccn.loc.gov/2018007458

A catalog record for this book is available from the British Library.

Special discounts are available for bulk purchases of this book.
For more information, please contact Special Sales at 410-516-6936
or specialsales@press.jhu.edu.

Johns Hopkins University Press uses environmentally friendly book
materials, including recycled text paper that is composed of at least
30 percent post-consumer waste, whenever possible.

Contents

Preface

Neither my father, who died in 2010, nor my mother ever had any interest in being called "locavores" or in participating in anything called a "food movement." But they always appreciated delicious homegrown food. That's a family trait I've inherited from both sides.

I'm a second-generation native Washingtonian, on my father's side. His father had come to Washington from his hometown of Atlantic City, New Jersey, to pursue a career in cooking. He was chef at the old Blackie's House of Beef, in Washington, DC. As a child, I didn't know much about his work, but my grandparents knew how to buy and prepare the best roasts, and we often had rich pineapple-bottomed cheesecake at Easter, which was apparently a secret Blackie's recipe. Our family visited Atlantic City almost every summer; we still do. It's a tradition to stop at roadside farm stands for fresh produce. Silver Queen corn used to be a favorite with my parents, along with fresh lima beans when we could find them. Today, my family usually gets a watermelon and loads up on blueberries.

My dad's mother owned a beauty salon on U Street NW, but she had come to the city decades earlier from Prince George's County, Maryland. When I was in elementary school, one of her brothers still farmed tobacco in Upper Marlboro—which we called "the country." Most summers, she made damson plum preserves, and cleaned, cooked, and froze (sometimes simply by setting them on the back porch, when winters used to be cold) mountains of greens and chitterlings in the kitchen at the back of their rented Adams Morgan row house. She always baked four cakes from scratch for the winter holidays— sour cream pound cake, coconut layer cake, German chocolate cake, and a yellow layer cake with chocolate icing, still my favorite dessert.

On my mother's side, we hail from a tiny crossroads in Marengo County, Alabama, called Shiloh. My mother and aunt discovered land records some years ago that showed property had been purchased by their great-great-grandfather, who was born around 1853 as the son of a white man and an enslaved woman. Years later when this forebear of ours got married, his father and former owner sold him the 65-acre parcel for one dollar, as he could not legally leave the property to his mixed-race son in post–Civil War Alabama. Extended relatives still live there on the wooded property they call "the old home place."

My grandmother grew up on that land but was living in Selma, Alabama, by the time my mom and most of her fourteen siblings were born. My mother jokes that my grandmother could be pregnant while cooking grits for breakfast, disappear into her bedroom for a few hours, then be back at the stove frying fish for dinner, with a newborn in her arms. During a family reunion in Selma several years ago, we walked on the historic Edmund Pettis Bridge. We also visited a barbecue joint that still smokes meat in the brick pit my mom's father built there, before moving the family to DC.

In 2001, after many years away, I moved back to Prince George's County, where my parents had been settled for twenty years. I began doing freelance work with chefs who were over the moon about the heirloom tomatoes, pastured eggs, and grass-fed beef they were getting through one-on-one connections with local farms. I was intrigued to find out that food like that was for sale to consumers at neighborhood open-air farmers markets in Dupont Circle and Takoma Park. I remembered shopping for fresh food from produce stalls and butchers on an almost daily basis while living in Mexico and Turkey, and I also had memories of the wholesale farmers markets my grandparents and parents used to shop at in DC. These new farmers markets were more orderly, maybe more limited in variety, and somewhat more expensive, but they offered an invitation to think differently about the way we were shopping and eating, which I thought was intriguing for consumers in the metro area in the early 2000s.

My parents rolled their eyes at my growing interest in this resurgence of local food while maintaining their own focus on the collard greens, zucchini, tomatoes, and green beans in my dad's garden. I myself suspected that "eat local" was just a marketing gimmick, maybe not very practical outside the orbit of white tablecloth restaurants. But as I started visiting farms and eating all the locally grown food I could find, my skepticism gave way to excitement and perhaps even obsession. I talked my friend, neighbor, and partner in all things food, Kristi Bahrenburg Janzen, into a month-long experiment in feeding our families entirely from local sources. It required a lot of planning and research to do that in 2005, but it worked out beautifully and sealed my commitment to the local food movement. Kristi and I shared our local food adventures with family, friends, neighbors, and others who were curious through our email newsletter "Local Mix" and a website we called "Real People Eat Local." Eventually these adventures led me to take over as publisher and editor of *Edible Chesapeake* magazine in late 2006.

Edible Chesapeake was one of about a dozen or so titles in the Edible Communities network at that time. As other media were not yet paying much attention to consumer interest in eating local and sustainable food, the Edibles were becoming the publications of record for local food communities. In my publisher's message for my first issue in March 2007, I wrote:

A couple of summers ago, my whole family discovered together how fabulous eating fresh could really be. On a lark, I challenged us to eat food sourced exclusively from within a 150-mile radius of our suburban Washington DC home for a month, and that "experiment" turned into a new paradigm of eating for us. I didn't realize it at the time, but the idea of eating locally was taking root in all of us. And for me, it was blossoming into a true passion.

We all looked forward to the road trips to farms to buy pastured meat, or visiting farmers' markets and learning how different varieties of tree fruits ripened serially through the season. My kids loved shucking fresh sweet corn and all of us loved eating it, boiled, grilled, or fried in local butter with pale, tender lima beans, onions and tomatoes. Milk in glass bottles became "that yummy milk" according to [my son] Louis. Catherine [my daughter] would bring her allowance money to the market to buy her own quart of plums or slab of farmstead feta.

After the month was over, we welcomed bananas, avocados and tortillas back to our table. But we had tasted local food, and it was good. We could never go back completely to our old ways. Eating locally is an approach to food that encompasses everything from gardening to gourmet, from fresh to kid-friendly, from healthy to hearty, and involves our entire family in a way that we all can embrace. I believe that every family, no matter how small or large, no matter how busy or economically challenged, can find a way to embrace eating locally at a level that works for them.

I thought publishing *Edible Chesapeake* would be a great way to continue writing about the food I loved and to provide an outlet for other local writers and photographers, while helping to win more converts to the local food movement. I envisioned spending many years publishing articles about the people, the ideas, the partnerships, and the foods that were changing the way we eat. More cooks and consumers than ever were at the tipping point for embracing the idea of eating locally and sustainably, but local food was still widely considered to be a novelty.

With Kristi as my managing editor and all the talented writers, photographers, illustrators, and experts who contributed to *Edible Chesapeake*, I focused on empowering consumers to overcome the perceived obstacles to eating fresher, more nutritious food. We wanted to change their thinking about what "food" could and should be. We shared a glimpse into the challenges facing farmers, grazers, market managers, chefs, food artisans, and food policy activists as they tried to anticipate and satisfy the growing demand for local foods.

We learned about the local food lexicon, such as the differences between grass-finished and grain-finished beef, why some farmers chose one or the other method, and what those choices meant for the environment and for consumer health. While we weren't yet using the word "equity" in the local food conversation, we wrote about some of the first efforts to bring farmers markets to economically disadvantaged neighborhoods and why some worked and others failed. We talked about the external costs of industrial food that keep mass-market prices low and about the true costs of producing healthy, sustainably grown local food. Throughout everything we published, we celebrated the joy of fresh, seasonal foods, and we celebrated the traditional foodways of Native American, African, and European people who found themselves here under vastly and sometimes cruelly different circumstances.

Edible Chesapeake was warmly received and widely distributed—forty thousand copies each quarter—from Frederick, Maryland, down to Hampton Roads, Virginia. But in the end, my writing background was not enough to prepare me for the challenges of being a magazine publisher, the one who is on the financial hook for a publication's success or failure. I felt similar to celebrated home cooks who were unable to translate their kitchen skills into financially successful restaurants. A business is very different from a vocation, and I gained a much deeper level of respect for everyone who runs a small business. After three years, I was overwhelmed by the unexpected demands of the magazine's popularity, as well as the financial strain of the recession on the fledgling local food economy that supported us. With a heavy heart, I closed the magazine in 2009.

But I couldn't let go of the food and agriculture community that I had become a part of. I was fortunate to be asked to join the staff of Future Harvest–Chesapeake Alliance for Sustainable Agriculture (CASA), where I worked for several years and got to know sustainable farmers and their successes and challenges in even more depth. I also had the privilege of serving on the boards of trailblazing local food organizations such as FRESHFARM Markets and ECO City Farms. My family and I continued to enjoy and explore the local food options that were expanding day by day. I watched the number of farmers markets double from 2007 to 2016, while rising consumer demand brought new questions about the scale of local food operations and about the social values that seem inherent in the farm-to-consumer connection; these values can be difficult to reconcile with the financial realities for both farmers and average- to low-income consumers.

How could we help farmers transition from growing commodity soybeans for sale to global processors to growing vegetables or raising beef for sale to local consumers? What could we do to make local food more affordable and accessible for people of all socioeconomic levels? How could we harness the resources needed—people, land, money, infrastructure, political will—to grow our fledgling local food system into a driver of sustainable economic, environmental, and social benefits?

The explosive growth of farmers markets has slowed in the last two years, here and across the country. But I've come to realize that farmers markets are just the tip of the iceberg of the local food system. Reaching a natural saturation point for farmers markets does not mean the Chesapeake local food economy is stalling or in trouble; it's just entering a new phase, like a teenager who has gone through a growth spurt and is now learning how to function in the world with a larger body, a wider reach, and a potentially greater impact. There is still a lot of growing up to do, growing pains to endure, and questions that need answers before our young local food movement truly matures into a sustainable local food system.

It has always kept me grounded to remember that my family, like a lot of families, has been eating local for a long time without thinking to call it that. I'm not sure a book like this one can exist without invoking this quote from writer-activist-farmer Wendell Berry, so often repeated because it is and always will be true: "Eating is an agricultural act." As thoughtful and well-informed consumers, we play an absolutely crucial role in increasing the demand for local food. But we must also help solidify community priorities and the business/political will to ensure that the local food system is inclusive and equitable for all.

This is a big idea, but it will take a lot of small ideas and actions to make it happen. It took decades to dismantle the preindustrial food system and it will take at least as long to rebuild a modern-day local food system. The point of this book is to empower you to know about all the ways you can help the local food system and to urge you to choose what you can reasonably do and enjoy doing it. It really is true that every little bit counts, more so when a lot of people are each doing a little bit. We are often encouraged to vote for local food with our dollars, but we can also vote for local food with our votes, by asking our elected officials at every level—from the school board to Congress—what they are doing to support smart, sustainable agriculture and healthy food policies within their area of influence. We can get involved through local food policy councils and nonprofit boards. We can make financial contributions to programs that expand access to healthy foods or help incubate community food businesses. We can grow our own gardens or become farmers ourselves. We need to engage at whatever level we can, if we truly want to regain control over what's on our plates.

In this book, I focus exclusively on what's happening in the local food system of the Chesapeake Bay region. Even more specifically, I ramble mostly across Maryland, DC, and Northern Virginia, but my network of producers and folks in the know extends to Pennsylvania, West Virginia, and all through Virginia's central, southern, and coastal regions. I have visited, bought from, eaten at, or met the owners of most of the businesses or organizations mentioned herein and been referred by reputation or a trusted local source to most of the others. By all means, visit and support any of the folks I talk about in *The Chesapeake Table*, but don't let my experience limit you. On the contrary, my experience should inspire you to seek out the farmers, fishers, and makers in your proverbial neck of the woods and determine for yourself, with whatever new insight you can take away from my writing, whether they should be part of your personal local food experience.

I made it my job, maybe even my personal crusade, to go out of my way and get deep in the weeds of eating local, so you don't have to. I've put what I know into these pages. All you have to do is read them and eat!

The Chesapeake Table

Introduction | Foraging in Maryland
Two Families Eat Local

RENEE BROOKS CATACALOS & KRISTI BAHRENBURG JANZEN

This article, an earlier version of which was published as "Suburban Foraging: Two Families Eat Only Local" in the August/September 2006 issue of *Mother Earth News*, describes what it was like trying to do a "150-mile diet" before the local food movement really took off. This experiment got me entrenched in the world of local food in the Chesapeake region, and it shows the lengths my friend Kristi and I were willing to go to for the cause.

A mid increasing media buzz about the virtues of local food, we set out to discover how feasible it is to eat only local food all the time. As two suburban moms, we wanted to know if "eat local" was just a hollow marketing slogan or a real alternative for families who hope to enjoy the best seasonal foods, invest in the local economy, and help the environment. How much would it cost? Would the kids go for it? Would our guests appreciate it?

Pledging to search locally for a month, we defined "local" as grown and produced within a 150-mile radius of our suburban Maryland homes near Washington, DC. We knew there were agricultural riches in our region. Yet much of what we discovered—or failed to discover—foraging in Maryland and the surrounding environs surprised us.

Enjoying Local Produce

Our own small gardens and those of friends and family were our start. They yielded zesty nasturtium blossoms for salads, hot chile peppers, edamame, sweet cucumbers, herbs, and other special produce. Renee's father had enough collards in his backyard to supply her all year. But, to feed our families of four, we needed a lot more.

1

We quickly became regulars at four producer-only farmers markets near our homes, where we picked up traditional favorites like corn on the cob, carrots bursting with flavor, mesclun greens, and various melons and berries. Kristi, eight months pregnant with her third child at the time, enjoyed the added convenience of weekly home delivery from two community-supported agriculture farms (CSAs).

By shopping at the farmers markets, we began to make new observations about our food. The taste of local tree fruits was particularly striking. While they are typically grown using some pesticides due to the humid mid-Atlantic climate, the flavor was far superior to any shipped from across the country, organic or not. Kristi couldn't stop craving local award-winning peaches and cream. The kids reveled in the fruit too, tasting new varieties like Metheny and Cardinal plums. Renee's husband, Damon, especially enjoyed the long run of fresh apricots.

Rounding Up Meat, Fish, and Dairy

We also tapped directly into the farming community. Kristi ordered Amish organic meat, dairy, produce, and other items such as maple syrup through a buying club with a biweekly delivery 30 minutes from home. Renee was in the habit of taking her family on bimonthly field trips to Springfield Farm in Sparks, Maryland, a one-stop shop of sorts, selling grass-fed beef and lamb, pastured pork, chicken, and rabbits, and fresh free-range eggs.

Sometimes, we turned to various co-ops and health food stores, although no single shop carried all the local goods we wanted. Between them, however, we found many dairy products—both cows' and goats', both certified organic and conventional—from dairies in Maryland and Pennsylvania. They also carried some local eggs, fruits, vegetables, honey, maple syrup, and a little meat. We were pleased to find that our local conventional grocery stores offered some locally grown produce as well.

The Chesapeake Bay region is well known for its seafood, but we didn't eat much of it during our experiment. Iconic products like blue crab and rockfish were simply too scarce and expensive. Renee had the occasional treat of a fresh croaker or two, a less famous but delicious regional fish, caught by her uncle, an avid sport fisher. Through her CSA, Kristi received some wild-caught Alaskan salmon, hardly local, but environmentally friendly.

The major challenges arose when we tried to find sources for pantry staples such as flour, rice, corn meal, oats, barley, cereal, lentils, dried beans, nuts, and dried fruit, as well as pasta and bread. Kristi did not eat much wheat while pregnant and was hoping to find spelt (a type of wheat that is low in gluten) or rye.

Wheat required a three-hour round trip for a rendezvous with Western Maryland farmer Rick Hood, who sold Renee a whole 10 pounds of wheat for just $2.50. We were stunned to find no commercial mills in Maryland grinding the millions of bushels of wheat and corn grown annually in the state. "The milling facilities in Maryland have died," Hood said.

With the help of a small kitchen grinder, Renee experienced the pleasure of baking with freshly ground wheat, although it required a lot of cleaning before grinding. She was relieved to eventually find Wade's Mill in Raphine, Virginia, via the internet. Millers Jim and Georgie Young stone-grind Virginia hard and soft wheat and happily fill mail orders with their old-fashioned twine-tied bags of flour. The only way to get local cornmeal was to drive to the tiny town of Westminster near the Pennsylvania border, where volunteers grind local corn at the historic water-powered Union Mills grist mill and sell it for $3 a bag.

Kristi was able to locate certified organic whole spelt and whole rye flour grown without pesticides, both from Small Valley Milling in Halifax, Pennsylvania. The spelt was also ground and hulled locally. "I probably have the only dehulling facility in Pennsylvania," said farmer and mill owner Joel Steigman, who knows farmers who send their spelt to Michigan for dehulling.

We were, however, unable to find any bakers using local grains. When Kristi asked one bakery representative where their grains came from, he replied with a baffled, "Is that a trick question?" As a result, Kristi supplemented with breads that were at least locally baked and Renee stuck to her homemade bread.

Maryland's Eastern Shore yielded pecans from 100-year-old trees at the Nuts to You farm, available every week at our local farmers market, as well as hybrid chestnuts from Delmarvelous Chestnuts, available by mail. Ground into flour, chestnuts pack a nutritional wallop and contribute to savory dishes like nutty-tasting crepes. Ordering nine jars of Virginia peanut butter online from The Peanut Shop of Williamsburg was probably the easiest purchase of the whole month.

As for legumes, we got them fresh all summer—edamame, crowder and black-eyed peas, baby lima and fava beans. Shelling the peas made the more finicky kids willing to at least give them a try. But we were told by more than one person in the know that the mid-Atlantic climate is not favorable for producing dried beans. And we were unable to find anybody offering the "grain, bean, and seed" CSAs that we hear are available in some parts of the country.

Trade-Offs

We never felt deprived by cutting out tropical fruits, frozen convenience foods, and typical snacks. The kids whined about their loss of cereal and pasta the first week, but as time went by, they got into the experiment (Laura Ingalls Wilder analogies helped!). They loved the open-pollinated Amish popcorn and homemade potato and sweet potato chips. To satisfy their craving for sweets, Renee made peanut butter cookies using maple sugar, while Kristi baked cookies with whole spelt flour and pecans.

We did spend more time than usual in food preparation, including some experimental baking. Renee made "graham nuts" cereal using a recipe off the internet in response to her five-year-old's plea for cereal during the last week. Kristi's week-long experiment making sourdough rye only yielded two edible loaves but piqued her interest in preparing the dark rye of her northern German ancestors.

Baking required us to make an exception to the 150-mile rule for leavening agents. We also granted ourselves additional exceptions, such as for oil and vinegar, salt and pepper, and tea. Kristi's husband, Bernd, couldn't do without coffee. Forgoing treats like refined sugar, chocolate, and spices was difficult. But we earned a profound new appreciation for globally traded flavor enhancers!

Wild Price Ranges and Hidden Costs

Price comparisons revealed that no one store was cheaper across the board. Price ranges of local foods were startlingly wide and defied stereotypes. Whole Foods—known in some quarters as "Whole Paycheck"—actually yielded some relative bargains, while the smaller health food stores, food co-ops, and farmers markets offered both bargains and sticker shocks.

To keep from busting our budgets, we watched for sales and limited the high-end gourmet stuff, such as artisanal cheese. By being a neighborhood

CSA coordinator, Kristi received her share of vegetables for free. We also made bulk purchases and grabbed seconds. Nob Hill Orchards, of Gerrardstown, West Virginia, for example, sells bulk berries at a discount, albeit frozen. Overripe peaches bought at half price from Harris Orchard, of Lothian, Maryland, made a fabulous crumble, and a half bushel of apple seconds for a mere $6 made quarts of fantastic applesauce.

Bulk discounts are especially valuable in purchasing meat. At Springfield Farm, rib eye steaks are $18 a pound and ground beef is $4 a pound, but Renee bought a 20-pound box of mixed roasts, steaks, and ground meat for $3.95 a pound. Whole steers, sides, or split quarters are as low as $2.50 a pound. "It really is a very good buy for people if they have the freezer space," said Valerie Lafferty, who runs the farm with her parents, David and Lilly Smith.

We intended to conserve fossil fuels by limiting the distance our food traveled to reach our tables. However, because the distribution system for local food is neither extensive nor coordinated, we did make lots of extra trips to pick up items from various suppliers. This was somewhat at odds with our intent, and we had to take the cost of gas into consideration.

At times, even though we paid a higher price for local food, we considered it a bargain. This was in part because the quality and flavor were so much better. But we also felt it worth paying more to help preserve small family farms and support locals who minimize environmental damage.

Putting It All Together

Eating locally allowed us to see the unique culinary possibilities of our region and taught us to stay creative and flexible in the kitchen. Sometimes, the vendor we were counting on didn't show up. Sometimes, supplies just ran out, or the weather brought crops to a premature end. Early on we learned not to get frustrated but let available foods lead the way.

In the process, we came to love the simple pleasures of seeing the kids eat three plums for a snack instead of cheese curls and making toasted cheese sandwiches with local cheddar on homemade bread. We also relished bringing gourmet meals to the table from our local bounty.

Kristi's French beef stew using Amish meat, her own herbs, local red wine, and bacon from Cibola Farms was the star of a dinner that included cabbage and tomato salad and spaghetti squash sautéed in butter, garlic, and onions. Family visiting from Montana enjoyed local breakfasts including French toast made with goats' milk and butter and spelt pancakes.

One of the favorites at Renee's house was her sausage ragout, made with sweet Italian or rosemary-garlic-lamb sausage, fresh tomatoes, sweet corn right off the cob, and whatever fresh pea or bean was in season. Real old-fashioned buttermilk became, and remains, a staple in her house for pancakes, scones, and cornbread.

At our end-of-experiment feast, everyone gobbled up award-winning goat cheeses from FireFly Farms, of Bittinger, Maryland, while sampling a variety of local wines and beer from Franklin's, a microbrewery just down the road from our homes. Dragon tongue beans, red peppers, shitake mushrooms, herbs, and pastured chicken thrown in a big pot produced a great stew. Blue potatoes, on discount at a local co-op, slathered in garlic and roasted, were a big hit with the kids.

Now that our one-month test is over, we've gone back to a few non-local items, like bananas and store-bought pasta. But we've retained a lot of our new habits, too. Once you get used to farm-fresh food, regular store-bought fare tastes remarkably bland. We're aiming to get more freezer space and planning to preserve more. We are really excited about the delicious fresh grain and bread-baking prospects too.

Perhaps even more gratifying, we've sparked conversations with local farmers and retailers about expanding the availability of local foods and introducing new products, such as bread baked with local flour. As we've turned many of our friends, relatives, and neighbors onto local food, we hope to see it become less of an adventure in foraging and more of an accessible choice for everyday eating.

Epilogue: Local Food Gains Ground

Nearly a year after our all-or-nothing experiment, both our families still rely heavily on our local foodshed. We don't deny ourselves the pleasure of tropical fruits or fair-trade coffee, but we buy local first and definitely purchase more local items than we used to.

The more we discuss local food, the more suppliers we discover. A conversation with the general manager of a neighborhood natural foods co-op, for example, resulted in higher-profile labeling of local products in the store. The bright yellow star that signifies "locally made" has led us to amazing discoveries, like tofu made from organic Virginia soybeans.

We've also found the general interest in local food to be widespread and growing. As many friends and neighbors continued to ask about our experiment, we recently hosted a neighborhood information session to share our months of research on local food. Thrilled to see more than forty people attend, we quickly ran out of the 6 quarts of pick-your-own organic blueberries we offered as a snack, along with Virginia peanut butter and homemade wild yeast sourdough bread. Folks were not only interested in our food sources but also wanted to hear how our children and husbands reacted to the local food, what our motivation was, and how we made it convenient and affordable.

We truly believe the more consumers seek local food, the more farmers will find it a viable economic opportunity, strengthening our local food system, local businesses, and communities all at the same time.

1 | Why Local, Why Now?

Remember the Life cereal ad that ran back in the 1970s with the two round-faced, freckled boys who made their younger brother, Mikey, try the new cereal that was "supposed to be good for you"? If not, look it up on the internet—it's a classic. Life cereal has nothing at all to do with eating local (although I like it, too!), but I feel as though I'm the Mikey of eating local. I tried eating local for all the "good for you" reasons, and not only did I like it, but the reasons turned out to be true as well. I jumped into local eating two-fisted, double-barreled, or whatever all-in synonym you like, and now I feel there are so many good and important reasons to eat local and benefits to be derived from doing it that I almost can't imagine why anyone wouldn't want to try.

But I have heard some of the reasons that people don't try, some of the obstacles people perceive to be in their way. The biggest ones tend to be a belief that eating local is only for the wealthy and a fear that it's too hard and time consuming. Others include intimidation because people feel they don't know enough about food or how to cook, or they simply don't know where to shop or where to start.

It can be hard to eat organic. Or gluten-free. Or low-fat. Or vegetarian. Or paleo. Or halal. Or kosher. But people do all these things and the food industry finds ways to support their efforts, for the most part. Similarly, eating local can present some challenges, but it is worth the small amount of effort it may require. If you have the will, you will find a way, and the more you know, the easier it will be.

The raw materials for local eating are all around us. Acres and acres of fields and pastures, orchards and forests, miles and miles of rivers and streams, ocean coastline, and the amazing Chesapeake Bay, all fashioned by nature to provide a full array of foods for people and all the other living things in our ecosystem. There was a time when *most food was local food*, whether people

Shoppers at the Baltimore Farmers Market under the Jones Falls Expressway. Photo by Aaron Springer.

lived on farms or in farming country or in the city where farmers brought their products from nearby to sell. Exotic foods such as olives, spices, and chocolate shipped in from other parts of the world were considered luxuries. Things have been turned upside down. Now, *most food Americans eat is shipped from somewhere else*, across the country or across the globe, and eating local is considered by some to be a luxury. It doesn't have to be that way, and the situation is starting to change.

Just over ten years ago, our local food scene began to gain momentum. What some—meaning the corporations shipping all that food—tried to dismiss as a fad instead became a movement, and now it is on the cusp of solidifying into an economically viable, sustainable, and inclusive local food system. In all corners of our region, there are passionate, smart, creative local farmers and food producers putting their bodies and souls—and sometimes their personal financial solvency—into cultivating and creating nourishing and delicious food, with the least impact to the environment and the shortest possible chain from its natural state. Everywhere there are committed professionals and experts at local nonprofits and government agencies working to develop the infrastructure, regulatory environment, political will, and regional collaboration needed to get this food to our plates. We also play a critical role. Consumers must be willing to make the deliberate choice to eat local, a little or a lot, in order for the local food system to thrive.

But what exactly is local food, and what is a food system?

The mildly frustrating news is that there is no universally accepted definition of local, either nationally or in our own region. But this is one of the very few situations when it's okay for everyone to determine their own definition of the word, because "local" as a distance modifier will always be a relative term.

Efforts to define what's local by city, county, or state boundaries is an unnecessarily limited exercise, given how close our mid-Atlantic states are to each other. Plenty of Marylanders live just across the border from farms in Pennsylvania, Virginia, or Delaware. Folks in southern Virginia may have an easier drive to a West Virginia or North Carolina farm than to one on their own state's shores of the Chesapeake Bay.

To determine what we would cover in *Edible Chesapeake*, we started with the Chesapeake Bay watershed and overlaid a 150-mile radius centered on Washington. The Chesapeake Bay is the anchor of our region's geography. Just as the flow of water down the many rivers and streams that drain into the Bay defines the Chesapeake Bay *watershed*, the journey of food from farms surrounding the Bay and from the Bay itself to consumers in Baltimore or Washington or Northern Virginia can help to define the *foodshed*. The agriculture of the entire region is also inextricably linked with the health and productivity of the Bay.

The Chesapeake Bay watershed actually extends all the way up into New York, but a 150-mile radius centered on Washington comprises virtually all of the watershed in Maryland, Virginia, and West Virginia, and a good portion in Pennsylvania. It also reaches out to areas of eastern Pennsylvania, southern New Jersey, and Delaware. It includes enough latitude to take advantage of different climate zones and topography that can produce a pretty complete diet, and we know that there is enough farming and fishing capacity within that radius to increase the amount of this food being sold to local consumers.

A 150-mile radius of where you live is a good way to define what's local for most people living in the Baltimore-Washington metro area, and I think it's more meaningful and practical than limiting yourself to a particular county or state. You can slide the bullseye or shrink the radius as you like, to create your personal foodshed to help guide your local eating.

A food system is made up of every step and resource involved in getting food from field, pasture, or water to the plate. It's been widely reported that food travels an average of 1,500 miles from farm to plate in America. Quick resources such as the Johns Hopkins University Center for a Livable Future's online Food System Primer and in-depth explorations of the industrial food system such as Michael Pollan's *The Omnivore's Dilemma* will help you understand how this disconnect came about. In fact, when it was first published

Map created for *Edible Chesapeake*. Hand-drawn by Mark Middlebrook.

in 2006, *The Omnivore's Dilemma* was a catalyst that prompted millions of people, including me, to start asking questions and taking responsibility for the food choices they were making.

A growing number of people believe that relocalizing food systems is one way to fix what's gone wrong with our food. Local food systems still cover all the steps of getting food from source to plate but are driven by four specific characteristics that distinguish them from the industrial food system: food security, proximity, self-reliance, and sustainability.

Food Security

In one sense, food security means safeguarding the biodiversity of our food sources so we always have the ability to grow more. The plants we cultivate for food come from plants that were once wild, were once just a few among infinite varieties of the same species, varieties that over the years adapted to various pests, weather, diseases, locations, and other pressures, to ensure their own survival.

Industrial agriculture has reduced the varieties of foods eaten by the vast majority of people in the world to just a handful. According to the United Nations Food and Agriculture Organization (UNFAO), five cereal crops—rice, wheat, corn, millet, and sorghum—provide 60 percent of the calories eaten, and a mere thirty crops total provide 95 percent of the calories of the world's population. Although more than five hundred banana varieties are estimated to exist in the world, nearly half of all bananas grown and virtually all bananas produced for commercial sale are of a single genetic variety called Cavendish, which many observers predict may actually be wiped out by a deadly disease that has taken hold of banana plantations. The UNFAO points out that local knowledge and traditional agricultural practices are key tools for increasing the security of food production through biodiversity.

When you compare the variety of fruits, vegetables, and animal foods produced by local farmers, you can readily see the role these farmers play in increasing biodiversity in the local food system. They choose plants that are resilient against pests, diseases, and our regional climate, and they experiment with different cultivars, both old and new, to bring different flavors and qualities of familiar foods to our tables.

Organic and other sustainable growing methods practiced by local farmers support biodiversity in many ways. Using seed that has not been genetically modified and even saving seeds from their own heirloom crops, farmers avoid reliance on plants that cannot evolve with the local environment. These and other practices provide protection against threats, natural or manmade, that can wipe out entire crops on which vast populations depend for their sustenance and livelihood. The devastating famine that hit Ireland in the nineteenth century had contributing political and social factors, but the underlying agricultural fact was that the country was dependent on a single variety for the majority of its staple crop of potatoes. Had there been other varieties, it's possible they could have been more resistant to the blight and would have survived. But the lack of diversity left the food system without the resilience to provide alternatives to the potato that was practically the entire diet for almost of half of Ireland's population, mainly the rural poor. Millions starved as a result.

Safeguarding our food supply in the event of emergency is another aspect of food security that can be uniquely addressed by the local food system. Grocery stores and wholesale food distributors use "just-in-time" supply systems that save them the cost of storing large quantities of products in their own facilities. This is more efficient in daily practice, but if trucking routes or

Faith, Farms, and Food Justice

Baltimore's Rev. Heber Brown III is a natural-born preacher, and he uses his talents to preach a particular message about food sovereignty in economically abandoned communities of color. As the young pastor found himself visiting many of his Pleasant Hope Baptist Church parishioners with diet-related illnesses in the hospital, he saw a need for education and action around healthier food. Rev. Brown walked the two blocks from his church to the Belvedere Square Market, where he found an abundance of beautiful produce and local food that was clearly out of reach financially for most of his congregation. He realized then that, although his church was not in a so-called food desert, "it was a 'food mirage'—we can see what we need, but we can't grab it."

To fix that, Rev. Brown transformed an empty lot owned by the church into a garden, growing produce for the congregation. For the first few years, they gave the produce away, then they started asking for donations, and now the produce is sold following church services. He has connected with local black farmers, such as Aleya Fraser of Black Dirt Farm on Maryland's Eastern Shore, to bring in larger quantities of produce,

creating an ad hoc food distribution network in neighborhoods in crisis following the arrest and death of Freddie Gray in 2015. Ultimately, he decided to tap into the landholdings of black churches, "the largest collective landholders in the black community," to foster the creation of the Black Church Food Security Network.

The Network addresses food security, personal health, social justice, economic self-sufficiency, and environmental justice through the deep roots of black church communities. With nine Baltimore churches actively growing their own food as well as supporting black-owned farms, a half-dozen more preparing to launch programs in 2018, and interest growing up and down the Eastern Seaboard, Rev. Brown's message has clearly resonated as a model for community-owned change. "We had all that we needed in the church to do what we needed to do."

Farmer Aleya Fraser and Rev. Heber Brown III with local vegetables for sale in Baltimore communities. Photo courtesy of Black Church Food Security Network.

power supplies are interrupted due to a weather or security situation, these just-in-time logistics can break down. The presence of farms within a closer distance could stabilize food supplies for short periods of time. A robust food system that includes local food processing capacity and facilities (also called food hubs) to aggregate local farm products for locally based distribution can be an even stronger bulwark against emergency food disruptions.

In the unlikely event that locally sourced food is implicated in a contamination or health scare, the short distance to the food's origins allows local farms to be quickly ruled out as the source of contamination or to be quickly identified for rapid containment of any outbreak. Locating consumers who bought a locally distributed product would be considerably easier and faster than the notifications possible with a nationwide recall.

Household food security—whether or not people can get enough food of sufficient quality and variety to maintain health—is another area where local food supplies can be part of the solution. A study by the Food Research and Action Center reached the conclusion, shocking in one of the nation's most affluent regions, that upwards of one in ten people in Washington, DC, Maryland, and Virginia may be going hungry for lack of access to adequate food. A 2016 study by Arabella Advisors, "Good Food For All: An Assessment of Food Systems Efforts in the Chesapeake Foodshed," concluded: "It is challenging to make local, fresh food accessible to those in high-poverty, high-unemployment neighborhoods without addressing the underlying economic and political drivers of poverty and economic insecurity. And those challenges are exacerbated by federal food policies that make commercially produced food—which is often less nutritious—the cheapest available option for the poor."

In addition to poverty and unemployment, the lack of grocery stores with fresh and healthy food options and the lack of reliable personal or public transportation to get to them contribute to food insecurity, and the situation is not confined to cities. The US Department of Agriculture (USDA) "food desert" map shows areas of low food access—more than ½ mile to a grocery store in urban areas and more than 10 miles to a grocery store in rural areas—dotting all of the region's cities but also covering large rural areas of Maryland's Eastern Shore and western counties, as well as many parts of central and southern Virginia. A study by the Food Desert Task Force in Virginia acknowledged that the local food system has the potential to offer solutions: "The Commonwealth of Virginia is known for impressive agricultural productivity, which suggests that food deserts and healthy food access issues are in

Crossroads Farmers Market in Takoma Park pioneered programs that match food stamps and Women, Infants, and Children (WIC) program benefits at farmers markets, now a feature of many markets across the country. Photo by Molly Peterson.

part a result of local and regional food distribution issues. With its abundant resources, Virginia has the potential to meet the needs of individuals living in food deserts and food-insecure households, while strategically strengthening agricultural markets and increasing access to healthy foods."

Some local solutions that can help include: community gardens where residents can grow their own food; farmers markets and community-supported agriculture (CSA) programs located in low-access areas where residents can shop using food stamps and Women, Infants, and Children (WIC) program benefits; and the distribution of fresh local produce through food banks. Enabling urban farms and cottage food businesses that can create jobs could also increase food security in these areas. Cohesive policies and funding could also make it easier to use local food resources to address hunger and food insecurity, for instance, through school and institutional purchasing.

Proximity

Proximity reduces the number of steps and the amount of time it takes to get food on our plates. One of the most important benefits of that shortened supply chain is the preservation of the nutritional value of our food. Nutrients in most plants begin to deteriorate the minute the produce is picked. A University of California study reported that produce grown in North America can spend up to five days in transit following harvest, followed by up to three days on a grocery store shelf. The report said that green peas lose 15 percent of their vitamin C and green beans lose 77 percent, after refrigerated storage for seven days. Fresh fruits and vegetables, picked when ripe and eaten shortly after harvest, enjoy an obvious nutritional advantage over produce harvested before maturity, subjected to potentially damaging handling and shipping, and stored for days or weeks, during which time the living enzymes and beneficial compounds are continually degrading.

Flavor benefits from being closer to the source as well. I have found this to be true with fresh eggs gathered just a day or two before eating, freshly caught seafood still carrying the brininess of Bay water, and all kinds of ripe fruits and vegetables. Local farmers actually grow particular kinds of strawberries, plums, melons, and other produce that can only be sold quickly and locally because they are too fragile to endure shipping and holding for any period of time, but they taste fabulous when picked and eaten right away. Produce available at local markets, farms, and restaurants can still bring that kind of immediate flavor to our tables.

We don't have to go to the hilariously ridiculous lengths of the TV show *Portlandia*'s earnest locavores who leave their restaurant table to check out the farm listed on the menu before placing their order. If we choose to, we can reasonably verify that the chickens at a farm 10 or 20 miles from our home do truly walk around on grass in the afternoon sun. We are close enough to visit the farms we buy from and see for ourselves that what the farmer has told us is true. If we are of a less suspicious nature, a farm visit is simply a wonderful way to affirm a connection with a local farmer and to remind yourself of the way that plants and animals grow before they become our food or drink. Observing the processes on a farm, seeing the scale of the operation, and

Fresh farmers market green beans.
Photo by Renee Brooks Catacalos.

Feeding Neighbors

In the uncertain days following the 9/11 terror attacks in 2001, neighbors living near Joan Norman's 172-acre One Straw Farm asked whether they could buy food from her if another attack halted interstate travel or caused stores to be shut down.

At the time, the Normans sold all of the production of their organic farm to wholesalers like Whole Foods Market. Thinking about the time her tomatoes, peppers, and eggplants spent on tractor trailers that hauled them miles away to be inventoried at a warehouse, just to be shipped back some days later to local grocery store shelves, she realized her food could get stuck at any point along the transportation chain, over which she had no control. She restructured her entire operation to focus on direct-to-consumer sales, creating the largest community-supported agriculture (CSA) program in the state. Today, One Straw Farm directly feeds about ten thousand people a week through a two-thousand-family CSA and sales to Baltimore restaurants and retailers, keeping most of its produce within a 40-mile radius of the farm.

understanding how many specific tasks have to happen before the food is ours also strengthens our appreciation of the farmers and farm workers who take such good care of our food.

Proximity allows farmers to build strong working relationships not only with consumers but also with local food processors, restaurants, retailers, policy makers, and others involved in the local food system.

Theoretically, there should also be a beneficial reduction in the use of fossil fuels associated with the transport of local food due to the proximity to markets. It's hard to prove, however, and hard to account for the effects of additional trips to farms, wineries, markets, and other outlets made by individual consumers in search of their favorite local products.

Self-Reliance

A strong local food system can help our region become more food self-reliant, producing more of the food necessary to sustain our own community. This puts greater value on the preservation of agricultural land as a policy priority and on food production as an attractive career path. But as pointed out in the Virginia food deserts study, farmers already produce enough food. Getting it to the people who want and need it, even in the local community, doesn't necessarily follow without deliberate focus and action.

The business connections forged through the interactions of local farmers, processors, retailers, and consumers circulate dollars back into the same community. Buying goods and services, related to food and otherwise, from fellow community members is the same as investing in the financial health of our town or state. Whichever side of the political fence you live on, we can all agree that keeping the community's dollars in the community creates a tide that raises all ships, whether it's through more prosperous businesses that are able to hire more workers, through people making living wages that enable them to buy more food and local products, or through government having the revenue to incentivize development in local food system infrastructure.

Self-reliance is the essence of farming, but today's American farmers are not subsistence farmers, trying to feed only themselves and their families from their labor. Modern farmers, including those farming organically and sustainably, are highly efficient. Yet the portion of every dollar spent on food in the United States that goes to the farmer actually fell in 2015 to 15.6 cents, its lowest point since 2006. Various case studies have suggested that farmers selling directly to consumers retain from 40 percent to as much as 75 percent of the food dollar, by shortening the number of intermediaries who take a cut of the price before it reaches the consumer. Selling high-quality food and value-added products within their community is a higher-margin business than selling their products wholesale into the commodity market to be combined with products from everywhere else and sold without regard to source.

Policies that promote the production and distribution of local food give farmers and small business people a chance to develop profitable enterprises with less regulation and red tape than might apply to larger businesses. We can get a high degree of accountability from a small business person who is known to us and has to face us if they don't live up to their promises, even if regulations don't require them.

Related on-farm agricultural businesses, such as creameries, wineries, breweries, and farm stores, can help increase a farm's financial self-sufficiency and bring high-value products to the community. The processes of small local food businesses involved in a short supply chain from source to table can be more easily verified and modified by local agencies than the operations of national and global corporations with inscrutable layers of hierarchy and endlessly linked supply chains.

Individual consumers also look to the local food system to help them gain more control over their food. The local food system has the potential to offer solutions for neighborhoods neglected by grocery stores, bringing opportunities to grow food and start food businesses that create jobs in the neighborhood, and giving the community ownership and a stake in the means of accessing good, healthy food.

Gardeners want to grow their own food, but they may also want to keep laying chickens in their backyard, just as their neighbors might keep cats or dogs. Individuals who understand the potential health risks associated with unpasteurized milk but feel that it's more wholesome, nutritious, and delicious than pasteurized milk, want to be allowed to purchase it from local farmers.

Consumers feel more self-reliant when they have more choices of where to spend their food dollars. Beneficiaries of programs like Supplemental Nutrition Assistance Program (SNAP, formerly known as food stamps) and the WIC program, or who receive emergency food assistance through food banks, would like fresh, healthy, and local choices as well. The local food system has the potential to give residents in all communities, including those that have been underserved or badly served by the industrial food system, an opportunity to be involved in planning and owning the means of producing food in their communities through community gardens, farmers markets, and food businesses that support community self-reliance.

Sustainability

Practically all of our environmental sustainability markers refer back to the Chesapeake Bay in one way or another. Water quality, air quality, agricultural productivity, livestock and fisheries management—all affect and are affected by the Bay.

In the local scheme of things, the Chesapeake Bay is the defining geographic feature of our region. Stretching 200 miles from the mouth of the Susquehanna River in the north to its union with the Atlantic Ocean in the south, the Bay is an estuary where fresh water mixes with salt water to create an especially fertile ground for aquatic life. More than fifty rivers and streams drain a watershed of sixty-four thousand square miles into this basin. The watershed covers all or parts of six states, with a combined population of more than seventeen million people.

In a global context, the Bay is one of the three largest estuaries in the world and the largest in the country. The Chesapeake Bay was once the most productive estuary in the nation. Over more than a century starting in the mid-1800s, the Bay yielded massive harvests of all kinds of seafood, but most notably oysters, crabs, rockfish, and a rarely heralded but critically important oily fish near the bottom of the food chain called menhaden.

By the 1960s, the Bay was teetering on the brink of ecological collapse.

Certified Organic pastured chickens at Ayshire Farm in Upperville, Virginia.
Photo by Kristi Bahrenburg Janzen.

The overfishing had long been unsustainable but was not being addressed in any meaningful way. Population growth hastened development, paving over farmland and open space that performed important absorption and filtering functions before rainwater reached the Bay. Runoff from chemical pesticides and fertilizers used on lawns as well as farms increased. Carbon emissions from vehicles and factories fouled the air and settled into the Bay as well. Industrial poultry production and monocropping of feed grains took over more and more acreage on the Eastern Shore, adding to the pollutants pouring into this sensitive body of water.

Today, the tide has been turned on damage to the Bay, although there is still far to go before experts will declare it fully restored. The rockfish, crab, and oyster fisheries, whose problems, ironically, were due to the global food system taking food out of our region rather than pumping it in, have been stabilized. Maryland and Virginia have had to work cooperatively to manage the Bay's fishing industries, including temporary or permanent shutdowns of parts of the Bay or its tributaries for certain species, along with tighter catch limits and shorter seasons to allow these populations to rebuild themselves. Aquaculture has also had a positive impact on the oyster market and has led

Author Renee Catacalos picks up a meat CSA share at Cabin Creek Heritage Farm in Upper Marlboro, Maryland. Photo by Louis Catacalos.

to a new emphasis on the unique characteristics of local oysters raised in specific parts of the Bay. Menhaden are still at risk from overfishing for industrial production of fish oil, and local food and environmental supporters must keep up the pressure on regulators to protect this humble but critical Bay species.

According to the website of the Chesapeake Bay Program, a regional partnership formed in 1983 to work toward the restoration and protection of the Chesapeake Bay, close to one-quarter of the land in the watershed is devoted to agricultural production, making agriculture the single largest source of nutrient and sediment pollution entering the Bay. The good news is that between 2009 and 2015, the levels of nitrogen, phosphorus, and sediment, key pollutants threatening the health of the Bay, decreased by as much as 20 percent.

Sustainable agriculture techniques practiced by small farmers in the local food system have had a major effect on reducing agricultural contamination. Produce and grain farmers can eliminate the use of chemical pesticides, herbicides, and fertilizers through organic growing methods or reduce them using techniques such as integrated pest management (IPM). These methods are also more sustainable for the farmers and farmworkers tending the crops because they reduce the health risks of exposure to agricultural toxins. Planting cover crops during the winter is another way farmers are restoring soil health. By using different species of crops, farmers replace the nutrients used by the cash crop during the season. Cover cropping also anchors the healthy topsoil needed for growing nutritious food and keeps that soil from running off into the Bay as a pollutant.

Livestock farmers also have an important relationship with the Bay. Water and soil quality is critical for these farmers who raise cattle, sheep, goats, bison, pigs, and poultry primarily on grass pastures. Likewise, grazing animals on permanent pastures restores the capacity of the land to absorb and filter water. The *Amazing Grazing Directory* of grass-fed meat, poultry, and dairy producers in our region says that permanent pastures have as much as 5 percent organic matter in their soils, compared to 1 to 2 percent in a typical cornfield. Every 1 percent increase in organic matter translates into the ability to absorb an additional thirty-two thousand gallons of water per acre. Other "best management practices," such as planting trees and installing fences to keep livestock out of waterways, also have a significant positive effect on water quality.

Eastern Shore farmers are beginning to see opposition to the construction of more and larger industrial poultry operations, and some groups hope to incentivize poultry and grain farmers to diversify into more sustainable options, much as Southern Maryland farmers have diversified out of tobacco over the past fifteen years.

Development is inevitable in the growing East Coast megalopolis. But it is neither inevitable nor desirable that development should mean a solid 100-mile-wide swath of paved urbanity from New York to Norfolk. Development can include a local food economy that makes farming a profitable-enough alternative that farmland and food production are seen as valuable parts of the mix.

Support from local buyers has helped to preserve a few farm oases just outside the Washington Beltway, such as Potomac Vegetable Farms on Route 7 in Fairfax County. Heyser Farms and Spicknall's Farm in Montgomery County still offer harried suburban drivers a pastoral vision of a field of strawberries or an orchard of apple trees as they near the end of their commute. Nonprofit and for-profit urban farms are sprouting up on previously vacant patches of land in Baltimore and Washington. These farms clean up and improve the soil of these abandoned lots and help urban residents establish connections to the local means of food production. Willowsford, a suburban residential community in Loudoun County, is built with a working farm as its centerpiece amenity.

Finally, financial sustainability cannot be overlooked as a key benefit of eating local. The farmers at your local market do not get a paycheck, pension, employer-sponsored health insurance, or paid time off. They are small business people who need to make more than they have spent on producing their products if they are going to support themselves and their families. If we don't buy from them at fair prices that honor their expertise and craftmanship, they will go out of business and we will lose the food choices they make possible.

It is well documented that local sales put more money in the farmer's pocket. When farmers and food producers do well, they create local jobs, generate local taxes, and reinvest their proceeds in services they buy from others in our community. Local money recirculating in local communities contributes to both community self-reliance and sustainability. It's kind of like the old rural tradition of barn-raising or the not-quite-so-old urban tradition of rent parties, except easier and with more in it for us. All we have to do is buy their delicious food.

Busy farmers markets offer a low-cost venue for incubating cottage food businesses, like makers of jam and candy, baked goods, pickles, and ferments. CSA programs are essentially a form of crowdfunding for small farms without access to traditional forms of financing, making consumers direct investors in the farm that grows their food.

When you buy from farmers and patronize restaurants and retailers who sell locally grown food, you also support a growing network of agricultural suppliers, local food aggregators, meat processors, and other related businesses. Even though lots of our local farmers enjoy small-scale farming, it's important for the local food economy to have farms of varying sizes to satisfy different needs in the market. It's also important for successful farmers who want to grow their business to have the means to do so without having to go outside the local food system. Having opportunities to diversify their products, explore multiple sales channels, and provide consulting services and specialized products such as organic hay and animal feed to other farmers are some of the local pathways to farm growth.

Experienced farmers, such as Jack and Becky Gurley in Maryland, Chip and Susan Planck in Virginia, and many others, also help sustain the local food system, by sharing their expertise with new farmers through programs such as the Beginner Farmer Training Program operated by Future Harvest–Chesapeake Alliance for Sustainable Agriculture.

Sustainable Food and Farming Organizations

Chesapeake Bay Foundation

http://www.cbf.org/issues/agriculture/

CBF supports land use programs and policies that slow the loss of farmland and prevent sprawl. Preserving farms and open space is essential, because these lands serve as precious natural filters for our water.

Fair Farms Maryland

https://fairfarmsnow.org/

The Fair Farms Campaign brings together consumers, farmers, public health professionals, and conservationists to advocate for visionary farming practices and support farmers who farm "against the grain" while protecting our waterways and our lands.

Future Harvest–Chesapeake Alliance for Sustainable Agriculture (CASA)

https://www.futureharvestcasa.org/

Future Harvest–CASA's mission is to provide education, networking, and advocacy to help build a sustainable Chesapeake foodshed, where food flows from farm and fishery to table in ways that strengthen farming and the regional food economy; protect our land, water, and air; and provide healthy, nutritious food that sustains the region's communities and cities.

Maryland Organic Food and Farming Association (MOFFA)

https://marylandorganic.org/

MOFFA is a nonprofit educational organization that brings together the community of growers, consumers, and retailers in Maryland to support organic and ecological farming and local food production.

Northeast Sustainable Agriculture Working Group (NESAWG)

http://nesawg.org/

NESAWG is a network of organizations and individuals carrying out farm and food systems endeavors in twelve states and Washington, DC, working to harness the power of a multisector regional network to catalyze meaningful change toward a sustainable and just food system.

Pennsylvania Association for Sustainable Agriculture (PASA)

https://www.pasafarming.org/

As the largest statewide, member-based sustainable farming organization in the United States, PASA seeks to improve the economic viability, environmental soundness, and social responsibility of food and farming systems in Pennsylvania and across the country.

Piedmont Environmental Council

www.pecva.org

The Piedmont Environmental Council works to safeguard the landscape, communities, and heritage of Virginia's Piedmont by involving citizens in related public policy and land conservation.

Virginia Association for Biological Farming (VABF)

http://vabf.org/

The Virginia Association for Biological Farming is the primary organization in the state of Virginia concerned with organic and biological farming and gardening.

Agriculture is a multi-billion dollar industry in both Maryland and Virginia, creating tens of thousands of direct and indirect jobs. The bulk of the industry is composed of the large-scale production of grains, soybeans, poultry, pork, and milk, commodities that feed into the globalized industrial food system. How much of the region's food production is actually being bought and eaten locally has been difficult to quantify. We know that it is only a small part of the overall food economy, but there are strong indications that plenty of room exists for both more locally grown supply and more local consumer demand.

In 2015, the USDA launched its first-ever Local Food Marketing Practices Survey to gather data specifically on local food sales. This survey recorded information about direct sales to consumers through farmers markets, on-site farm stores, roadside stands, CSAs, online sales, pick-your-own operations, mobile markets, and the like. It also counted direct sales from farms to local retailers, restaurants and caterers, and institutions such as hospitals and schools and through "intermediated" channels like local food processors or food hubs that aggregate and market local products sourced from many farms to larger local buyers.

The survey reported $8.7 billion in local food sales nationwide. It reported $217 million in local food sales in Virginia—the ninth-highest total in the nation, behind lots of big states as well as the tiny locavore superstates Vermont and Massachusetts—and $84.3 million in Maryland. Making an imperfect comparison using the most-recent data we have for total agricultural sales counted by the 2012 Census of Agriculture, direct local sales represented about 2.2 percent of total sales nationally, with 5.7 percent for Virginia and 3.7 percent for Maryland. All of these percentages probably overstate the case a bit, since overall agricultural sales in 2015 are almost certainly higher than they were in 2012. However imperfect, they still seem to indicate that farmers are selling more food locally in our region than across the country and that our Chesapeake local food economy is relatively strong.

I noted in the preface that the number of farmers markets and CSAs had leveled out in the last few years. The Local Food Marketing Practices Survey shows that flat numbers for those sales channels do not mean that the demand for local food has been satisfied. Rather, it shows that more farmers markets and CSAs alone are not the whole answer.

For instance, I live within a convenient distance of four farmers markets that I could shop at on a weekly basis, two of them all year-round. But three of them are open at the same time on Sunday morning. So, even having four local farmers markets, I still have just two four-hour time periods in which to shop each week. Although CSAs that deliver, sometimes directly to your doorstep, can be very convenient, it still can be a challenge for all but the most committed locavores to face properly storing, cooking, and eating a week's worth of vegetables that appear all at once, making the market for CSAs somewhat self-limiting.

It's most likely that farmers market and CSA growth has stalled because those modes of getting local food have reached equilibrium with the customers who want them, at least for the moment. Consider that the massive Baltimore Farmers Market under the Jones Falls Expressway has eight thousand shoppers on peak Sundays. In a city of 650,000, you'd need more than 80 farmers markets of that size to get everyone in on the action. There are currently only about twenty farmers markets within the Baltimore Beltway, and no others get anywhere near eight thousand shoppers a week. Neither CSAs nor farmers markets will ever be the whole answer if we want to increase the market share of local food by even a single percentage point. But the smart people in our local food system know that. They are building it, and we must come.

Easy Applesauce

I try to make applesauce at least once every fall. More of a technique than a recipe, it's quite easy, but it does take some time. Peeling and coring the apples before cooking them, rather than cooking them all together and then straining the peels and cores out, results in a chunkier applesauce that's ready to eat as soon as it's cooked.

Prepping the apples is a great activity for a Sunday afternoon of watching football or movies, and it's even better if you've got a kid, spouse, or friend to help. I like to use Gala apples because they make a sauce that is sweet without adding any sugar, but feel free to use more-tart cooking apples or a combination of varieties to suit your taste. Look for opportunities to buy apples by the half-bushel (around 60 to 65 medium apples) or bushel (around 125 medium apples). Fruit that is oddly shaped or a bit dinged up is sometimes labeled as "seconds" and sold at a discount, which is good value for making applesauce. You can easily scale up the recipe below, but you might want to enlist a friend to help. It takes a while, but opening a jar of homemade applesauce in February is worth it.

12–14 medium apples—Gala or a mix of
Gala, Idared, Cortland, or other cooking apples
Juice of 1 large lemon
1 cup water
1–2 cinnamon sticks

Quarter, core, and peel the apples. Place them in a large stock pot, squeezing the lemon juice over them as you go. When all the apples are in the pot, add the water. Place the pot over medium heat. Once the water starts to simmer, stir the apples in the pot every few minutes, breaking them up as they soften. Add the cinnamon stick after about 20 minutes, when more than half the apples are cooked and mushy. Continue simmering for another 20–30 minutes, stirring frequently until sauce consistency is reached, depending on the firmness of the apples you've used. Remove the cinnamon stick after cooking.

You can mash the apples with a potato masher if you want to break up the chunks further. If you want to preserve your applesauce, follow canning instructions from your favorite cookbook or the *Ball Blue Book of Canning*. If you want to enjoy it in the short term, cool the applesauce, ladle into jars, and store in the refrigerator for up to a week. Makes about 2 quarts.

2 | Tastes of the Region

Restaurants have been aware of the cache of local sourcing and farmers market shopping for years. Locally grown produce ranked second in 2006 on the National Restaurant Association's "What's Hot, What's Not" trend survey of more than one thousand chefs nationwide. In 2017, basic local sourcing had become such a given that three of the top ten spots on the list went to subsets of local sourcing: hyper-local sourcing (for example, restaurant gardens, house-made charcuterie and in-house brewing); locally grown produce; and locally sourced meat and seafood.

Restaurants Showcase Local Food

Chefs were the tastemakers who opened the door for the growth of the local food system in the Chesapeake. Restaurants are a great place to try new things, see how they can be elevated to their finest form, and get inspired to see what you can do with them at home, even if you can only afford to eat at the really progressive restaurants a couple of times a year.

I owe my introduction to the entire idea of eating local to one of the very early farm-sourced restaurants in Washington, DC. As a communications consultant to Todd and Ellen Gray at Equinox Restaurant in the early 2000s, I got a crash course in farm-to-table, knowing very little at the time about the way either farms or high-end restaurants worked. One of my most incredible experiences was a tasting of Randall Lineback veal, a rare American seventeenth-century breed of cattle being saved from extinction by creating a culinary market for the meat. With my five-year-old daughter Catie in tow, I was among the group that ate this heritage breed for the first time in perhaps hundreds of years, as Todd and his kitchen staff tested the flavor, texture, and tenderness of each of the cuts they had prepared while determining how best to feature them on their menu.

Hen Quarter's fried blue crab fingers are one of many locally sourced dishes on local restaurant menus. Photo courtesy of Hen Quarter.

Todd received deliveries from Tuscarora Organic Growers Cooperative, a group of small organic vegetable growers in Pennsylvania who formed a cooperative to market and transport their produce to DC chefs. Ellen organized tasting events featuring Virginia wines paired with local foods, when there were far fewer good Virginia wines to feature. They held quarterly dinners to mark the changing of the seasons with expressly local menus. I still have vivid and tasty memories of Todd's crispy soft-shell crab at one of those dinners, two dainty backfin lumps with crunchy tendrils that looked not very much like legs at all.

But all this dreamy food play was thanks to my job. I knew that, in real life, I couldn't afford any of it, but that didn't mean I didn't want it or think I should be able to have it. That's what inspired me to wonder whether I could find ingredients like this to cook for myself. Clearly, I was not going to get the rarest beef in the country for my home kitchen, but there were farmers raising other breeds in a similar way, so I felt I should at least be able to buy quality local meat that had a traceable source.

I might never have asked the question if I hadn't been exposed to the possibility. Along with other well-known chefs such as José Andrés, Cathal

Armstrong, Jeff Black, Ris Lacoste, Rob Weland, and Nora Pouillon (who retired and closed her groundbreaking eponymous restaurant in 2017), Todd Gray helped stoke the wave of local food interest in DC, with more excellent restaurants continuing in that vein.

But farm-to-table is not limited to white tablecloth and Zagat-rated establishments. The Clyde's Restaurant Group has long been committed to local sourcing, with little or no fanfare. Ype Von Hengst, owner and executive chef of the Silver Diner chain of mid-priced restaurants, spent $1 million to completely restructure his company's purchasing and menus, creating relationships with larger local and sustainable sources of eggs, beef, poultry, and seasonal ingredients, proving that restaurants at various scales could source locally.

Ahead-of-the-curve restaurants outside DC that are still carrying the farm-to-table banner include Tuscarora Mill and the Restaurant at Patowmack Farm in Loudoun County, Virginia; Ricciuti's in Olney, Maryland; Restaurant Eve and Vermilion in Alexandria, Virginia; Gertrude's in Baltimore; and many more than I can list here. Spike Gjerde's Woodberry Kitchen and its spinoff enterprises in Baltimore and DC have become a micro food system in and of themselves, with vertical integration in-house of many parts of the process from butchering, to curing and charcuterie, to freezing and canning produce during peak growing seasons, to private-label jams and hot sauces, all from local farm ingredients. Restaurants with their own growing operations, not just kitchen gardens but full-fledged farms with fields and greenhouses and separate farming staff, are another increasing trend that shows a desire to ensure an ongoing supply of local ingredients for their kitchens.

The Baltimore-Washington corridor is one of the most racially and ethnically diverse areas of the country, according to various publicized studies. Ours is also a super-diverse culinary scene, of which farmhouse or New American cuisine is a relatively small part. I remember reading this passage in one of Todd Kliman's reviews for the *Washingtonian*, about the Howard County restaurant Ananda: "The owners manage a small farm not far from the restaurant, and you can taste the literal fruit of their labors in an elegant squash soup. If you're thinking, 'Yeah, so? Don't a lot of restaurants use products from local farms?,' allow me to share a crucial piece of information: Ananda is an Indian restaurant."

I talked to Todd, who has eaten in as many restaurants throughout DC and its suburbs as anyone, about whether more ethnic restaurants are using locally sourced food. Restaurateurs from countries where the industrial food system is not as dominant as it is here often don't anticipate this conversation. Locally sourced food is still the default in many places around the world. Todd told me about the owner of an Ethiopian restaurant that we both know and love who looked into sourcing local a few years ago. "They wanted to do free-range chicken. They said the taste of chicken here is different because in Ethiopia, all the chicken is free-range." But they found that the price difference would have cut out a large part of their clientele, as the American eating public has developed the expectation that ethnic food is going to be inexpensive.

It's not possible for me to list all the restaurants worthy of your notice for their local sourcing here. Not all restaurants tout their local sources, either. Ironically, as more channels for local farmers to sell their food through cooperatives or distributors emerge, there may be less awareness on the part of restaurants when the product they receive has actually come from a local farm (more on that in chapter 5). But I encourage you to ask about sourcing at your favorite restaurant or ask your favorite farmers which restaurants they sell to.

Sampling the Landscape

Another fun way to get into local foods is through sampling events and tourism around food and drinks. You can get an idea of the array of local foods and beverages through special events and tastings. There are seventeen wine and distillery trails in Virginia and nine wine trails in Maryland, including a cider trail and a mead trail. Be sure you have a designated driver before you set out on one of these explorations! The same goes for wine, beer, and spirits tastings. Even with thimble-sized tasting cups, I found that I had to stop after visiting two or three booths at a Maryland Distillers Guild event. My sister and I were very grateful for the informative sessions with local distillers where we could sit down and listen to fascinating facts about local liquors for a few minutes, before taking another run at the samples!

Maryland also promotes an ice cream trail of nine dairies selling homemade ice cream, and the Virginia oyster trail throws in a little bit of everything, anchored around the locations of oyster farms and restaurants. Wineries, breweries, and distilleries offer all kinds of music festivals, farmers markets, and other activities that make it easy to go out and spend the whole day while getting familiar with their various products. Other ways to

Grilled cowboy rib eye at Liberty Delight Farms in Baltimore County.
Photo by Michelle Scholtes.

experience local foods and try before you buy include festivals that celebrate crabs, oysters, apples, and other foods; county fairs, farm heritage festivals, and food events at museums and historic homes; and chef-driven themed dinners at restaurants, on farms, and on rooftops that celebrate Chesapeake ingredients and flavors.

On the Table Every Day

Once you have a taste of what's possible, you will probably be inspired, if you enjoy cooking, to seek out local foods to cook and eat at home. If your local farmers market is only open during the growing season, you might think that eating local at home is also limited to the growing season. Not true. We can celebrate the seasonality of farm-fresh foods, but still enjoy locally produced food year-round using both old and new methods. There is a certain warm satisfaction in being able to put local food on the table any time of the year.

Dehydrating, canning, and fermenting are tried and true. If you don't want to "put up" food yourself, local farmers and makers produce plenty to line your shelves. Freezing makes it even easier to preserve some of summer's harvest ourselves and is a boon to local meat producers who can keep

A young visitor learns to love salad in a hoop house at ECO City Farms.
Photo by Sonia Keiner.

meat on hand throughout the year. Greenhouses, hoop houses, hydroponics, and aquaculture mean some types of produce, fish, and shellfish can be produced fresh continually. Committed consumers in the Chesapeake region can find locally produced food, without growing a single lettuce leaf themselves, 365 days a year.

Farmers grow a variety of crops indoors using either permanent greenhouses or hoop houses, which are temporary structures covered with heavy plastic used to cover field crops during cold weather. Most of these crops—cherry tomatoes, salad tomatoes, cucumbers, basil, lettuce, arugula, spinach, microgreens, pea shoots—are grown in soil, but some farmers use hydroponics systems, which replace soil with nutrient-fortified water. Tender lettuces such as butter, romaine, and red oak are well suited to hydroponic farming. Cultivated mushrooms such as shiitakes and oysters are grown almost exclusively indoors and are available all through the year.

Most apple farmers have cold storage that maximizes the availability of apples through the winter and into late spring. There might be a one- or two-month gap between the end of the storage apples and the appearance of the fresh Ginger Gold apples in late summer, making them the only local fresh fruit that you can count on just about year-round.

Jam, jelly, tomato sauce, applesauce, fruit butters, dried apples, and dried herbs are common at farmers markets, where they are sold by the farmers who grew the produce. Farm stores may have more "canned" fruits and vegetables, which are more likely to be in jars than cans. Although some farms "put up" produce they grew themselves, others process produce they buy from farmers who may or may not be local. Take the time to read the labels and ask some questions to find out as best you can whether the ingredients in the jar were actually grown locally.

Homemade pickles, sauerkraut, kimchi, and other products made by fermenting fresh vegetables are very popular. The naturally occurring bacteria present in these foods have probiotic benefits, and local producers seem to be having fun infusing traditional recipes with interesting new combinations of herbs, spices, and other flavorings. These are available throughout the year, either canned or refrigerated, but the raw ingredients change based on seasonal availability.

Fresh local pastured chickens are usually only available at farmers markets from spring to fall, but some farmers bring frozen chicken to market in winter. Stores that source locally (see list in chapter 5) have fresh chicken all year-round and usually also have a steady supply of local eggs, even when they become scarce at farmers markets during the winter. Beef, pork, and bison are more readily available from stores, farmers markets, farms, and local food delivery services all through the year. The supply of lamb is a little less reliable but still pretty consistent.

Local milk, cheese, yogurt, butter, and ice cream from small-farm dairy cooperatives such as Trickling Springs and Natural by Nature, both located in Pennsylvania, and Homestead Creamery, located in Virginia, are staples at stores that source locally as well as larger chains such as Whole Foods. Local cheeses made from the milk of cows, goats, and occasionally sheep, ranging from everyday cheddars and fetas to artisanal blue cheeses and soft washed-rind camemberts, mean you can put together an impressive cheese tray for summer wine and cheese, New Year's champagne toasts, or school-year PTA meetings, from the farmers market or well-stocked local cheese shop.

Thanks to modern aquaculture, clams and oysters are on the menu in all seasons, even in the months ending in "r" that used to be taboo because of the oyster spawning season. Striped bass, known in the Chesapeake Bay as rockfish, and other fish, including black bass, flounder, sea trout, catfish, and

Pantry Staples

The foods we most think of as pantry staples—grains, rice, and dried beans—can be the Achilles heel of eating local in our region. Wheat has been grown here since colonial times, but commercial mills moved to the Midwest to be closer to the center of industrial grain production and by the mid-twentieth century, wheat and corn farmers in Maryland and Virginia were sending their harvest out-of-state for milling.

That was the situation during my 2006 local eating experiment, when Rick Hood of Summer Creek Farm agreed to sell me 10 pounds of wheat that would have otherwise gone to a nearby mill to become part of a nice, but not identifiably local, bag of flour. You can now find corn meal, wheat flour, and sometimes other products, including buckwheat or rye flour, at farmers markets from producers such as Homestead Farms of Faulkner, Maryland, and Frederick's Full Cellar Farm, which will mill your grain for you while you wait. Many historic mills sell stone-ground corn meal, grits, and various types of flour, but their grains are not always from local sources. Rob Moutoux experimented with growing grains on his Loudoun County, Virginia, farm when he and his wife Maureen launched their whole-diet CSA, a kind of farm share that aims to provide the bulk of a family's vegetables, fruits, meats, dairy, eggs, and flours. But he soon found "there were too many production elements involved to do it well with everything else on the farm." He ultimately switched to providing a variety of grain flours sourced from Frankferd Farms in Pennsylvania to his CSA members.

Most locally milled wheat flour is soft wheat, best for biscuits, cookies, pie crusts, and quick breads. Local bakers who need higher-gluten bread flour often work with Pennsylvania companies such as Daisy Organic Flours or Small Valley Milling, which produces organic spelt flour, or Anson Mills in North Carolina, to get commercial-quality flours with some local grain content.

Heinz Thomet at Next Step Produce in Newburg, Maryland, grows wheat, rye, barley, and oats. He is also the first farmer known to grow rice in the Chesapeake region since

Hoppin' John with rice and black-eyed peas from Next Step Produce. Photo by Renee Brooks Catacalos.

perhaps the 1880s. Since 2011, he has cultivated a Japanese variety of "upland" or "dry-land" rice that grows without the need to flood the fields. According to the farm's website, "When we were asked, 'Why grow rice?,' the answer was: 'Because we eat rice.'"

Nazirakh Amen of Takoma Park's Purple Mountain Organics has collaborated with Che Axum at the University of the District of Columbia's Muirkirk Research Farm in Beltsville, Maryland, to do agricultural trials on the rice being grown by Thomet, as well as other potential dry-land varieties. The goal of the project is to see if rice could be grown in urban areas like DC. Early on, they were able to double the yields achieved by Thomet and produce enough to land it on the menu at Takoma Park's Republic restaurant. I sampled the rice at a farming conference one year and wanted to buy more, but Amen protested with a smile, "They [Republic] buy everything I can grow!" Thomet's rice and other grains, as well as a few varieties of dried beans, are available through his farm and at Chesapeake's Bounty in St. Mary's and North Beach.

the invasive blue catfish are fished most of the year. Pasteurized crabmeat is an all-year staple, and many of the fish caught locally are available frozen or smoked at any time.

Sweeteners such as honey and maple syrup are only harvested during certain seasons. Maple producers and larger apiaries bottle enough to keep up a year-round supply, but farms that bottle honey as a sideline from their main produce operations may run out by winter. You can also get regional salt, harvested by J. Q. Dickinson, a seventh-generation family salt business, from an ancient salt ocean trapped beneath the Appalachian Mountains.

Vegans are often surprised to learn about organic tofu from Twin Oaks Community Foods, a worker-owned cooperative in Louisa, Virginia. Their tofu and other soy products are available at many natural food stores in the area. On a shopping trip to Chesapeake's Bounty in North Beach, Maryland, I learned that a Pennsylvania company, Susquehanna Mills, makes cooking oils from locally grown sunflowers, rapeseed/canola, and hemp.

If you enjoy alcoholic beverages, you can choose from award-winning wines, ciders, meads, beers, and distilled spirits made with local fruits, grains, and other seasonal ingredients. Sample them at tasting rooms or festivals, have them at restaurants, or buy them to experience at home. As more local beverage operations come online, more and more wine and liquor stores are

Small apiaries and hobby honey farms make local honey a great option for gift giving and for everyday use. Photo by Renee Brooks Catacalos.

carrying them on their shelves. Check the websites of your favorite beverage producers for a list of stores that sell their products.

Spring Flavors

Astronomical spring actually starts on the vernal equinox in late March, when the hours of the day, slowly lengthening through the winter, finally equal the hours of the night. Spring continues until the longest day of the year, the summer solstice, three months later. The warmth on the breeze as the days get sunnier makes us antsy for fresh foods, but the winter wait is not quite over. Those who garden are more in tune with the need to temper expectations. They know that the ground is just starting to thaw in March, so it's really planting season, versus eating season. But March turns to April, and April, eventually, brings strawberries.

Strawberries can last through June, if the weather cooperates, and are often joined in markets by rhubarb, which is a vegetable so often cooked with strawberries that most people think of it as a fruit. These two have the fruit stage all to themselves for several weeks, until June, when blueberries, cherries, red raspberries, and black raspberries begin to ripen.

Asparagus is spring's first vegetable. It is the tender shoot of a plant that grows tall and fern-like when allowed to mature. Garlic scapes and spring onions are also shoots available only in early spring, before the garlic and onion plants start putting their energy into building up the bulbs under-

Local Food Directories

These all-purpose directories are good places to start searching for a farm, CSA, or farmers market or to get an overview of what's available in a certain area. Look for other directories for specific types of products or businesses in chapters 3, 4, 5, and 6.

Buy Fresh Buy Local
A nationally recognized program working to promote locally grown food to the public, connect consumers to local food producers, and change local food priorities:

Buy Fresh, Buy Local Chesapeake
http://www.cbf.org/join-us/more-things-you-can-do/buy-fresh-buy-local/
The only chapter in Maryland began in 2006 with a volunteer group of farmers, restaurateurs, and local food advocates. The Chesapeake Chapter is now administered by the Chesapeake Bay Foundation (CBF).

Buy Fresh, Buy Local Virginia
https://www.buylocalvirginia.org/
The Piedmont Environmental Council (PEC) launched Virginia's first Buy Fresh Buy Local campaign in 2006 and today manages nine Buy Fresh Buy Local chapters throughout the state of Virginia.

Maryland's Best
http://marylandsbest.net/
The Maryland Department of Agriculture's consumer guide to farms and products, including seafood, with a searchable database of farms, producers, and farmers markets; an interactive map; and video features about Maryland farmers.

USDA Local Food Directories
https://www.ams.usda.gov/local-food-directories/onfarm
Databases of farmers markets, CSAs, on-farm stores, and food hubs can be filtered by state, including the District of Columbia, and are available in English and Spanish.

Virginia Grown
http://www.vdacs.virginia.gov/vagrown/
The Virginia Department of Agriculture and Consumer Services consumer guide lets you search by region for farms, farmers markets, CSAs, and products made in Virginia.

ground. Spring is also the season for cool-weather field crops such as spinach and arugula, broccoli and cauliflower, beets and cabbage, radishes and sweet peas. Their sharp, bright flavors brighten our palates and our moods. You might also discover foraged delicacies, including fiddlehead ferns, morel mushrooms, and the red-stemmed wild leeks called ramps.

Farmers who started new flocks of chickens in early spring have fresh chicken available by April or May. Eggs from small flocks become more plentiful and the yolks become more deeply colored as hens get back on fresh pasture.

Bony fish good for frying, such as croaker and spot, come into season. Hard-shell blue crabs become available by Memorial Day, but the spring star of the Chesapeake Bay is the soft-shell crab. Though some are caught just after molting, most soft-shells are caught when they are about to molt and maintained in "peeler" tanks so crabbers can sell them the minute the shell is gone. Soft-shells are prepared and eaten whole, with minimal gutting and removal of just a few inedible parts. After my first experience with Todd Gray's elegant soft-shell presentation, I was a little taken aback the first time I saw them in a sandwich, with crispy fried legs hanging out between the slices of white bread. I've since tried these undressed crabs in many different preparations. Biting through the thin, papery almost-shell to the firm, sweet meat inside is a unique experience that I have come to appreciate.

Summer Bounty

The promise of spring is fulfilled in summer, running from the solstice in late June through the autumnal equinox at the end of September. During these hot and sunny months, we look forward to cooling off with fruits and vegetables that are refreshing and thirst quenching. Everything starts ripening and coming to market at once. If the team color of the spring market is bright green with a strawberry red accent, summer markets proudly display every color of the rainbow.

All manner of berries start to appear as June turns into July—blueberries, blackberries, red and black raspberries, gooseberries, and sometimes elderberries and currants, too. Early summer is a great time to visit a pick-your-own berry farm, before the weather is too humid or hot. Cherries are abundant and other tree fruits come into season—figs, more varieties of plums than you knew existed, nectarines.

July marks the apex of summer produce—pole, snap, and lima beans; black-eyed and crowder peas; multicolored carrots, radishes, onions, and new potatoes; chard, collards, and mustard greens; peppers—hot and sweet, red and green, yellow and purple; okra, zucchini, yellow crookneck and two-toned zephyr squash, and eggplants, so many eggplants. And of course, the stars of summer: white, yellow, and bicolor sweet corn, and field-ripened

Rainbow colors grace farmers markets in high summer. Photo by Renee Brooks Catacalos.

tomatoes of impossible-to-imagine shapes, sizes, and colors, lining farmers markets as far as the eye can see.

And just when you think it can't get any better, or hotter, August offers up the first of the peaches. Peaches, maybe more than any other tree fruit, seem to be exponentially better when tree ripened and freshly picked than in any form in which they can be preserved. Whether eaten out of hand, sliced up over ice cream, or baked into a cobbler or an open-faced galette, the magic of local peaches is not a myth. August also brings watermelons, cantaloupes, and more melons of all kinds, which grow famously well in the sandy soil of the Eastern Shore. There are early apples, more greens, tomatoes, cucumbers—basically more of everything. Those who "put up" for winter are busy, busy, busy.

Small beekeepers bring the year's fresh honey to market in summer. It's the height of the season for hard-shell blue crabs, and fish species such as mackerel, drum, bluefish, and ray are also more plentiful.

The Freezer Is Your Friend

The bounty of summer and fall can easily overwhelm you if you look at all that food and think you have to eat it immediately. Learning to make your freezer your friend and investing in a larger one if you can afford it, is one of the best steps you can take to get the full value out of local food.

A surplus of greens in the CSA box is a common complaint I hear from people. My mother's approach to greens, whether they came from my dad's garden, the farmers markets, or the grocery store when they are plentiful and on sale, has always been to cook them and freeze them.

She doesn't let a bunch of greens sit around—she attacks them right away, washing them thoroughly in the sink and cooking them in a huge pot, usually with a piece of pork, in the tradition true to her Alabama roots. Once they are cooked and cooled, she ladles them into gallon-sized freezer bags, including the liquid they are cooked in (called pot likker in the South, if you didn't know), and stacks them in the freezer. They are ready to be thawed and reheated at any time, and usually there would be enough in the freezer by the end of fall to last through the winter.

Fall Harvest

Fall is called the harvest season because that's traditionally when farm families would bring in the long-growing grains such as wheat, oats, and corn for milling or storage and dig up all the root vegetables to cure and fill their root cellars for the winter. It runs from the autumnal equinox to the winter solstice. Harvest season begat harvest celebrations like Thanksgiving and the idea of overflowing cornucopias of food.

Fall is the best time to appreciate our long heritage with apples, as scores of different varieties make their appearance as they ripen in succession. Fresh sweet cider is a fall treat (as are apple cider donuts!). This is also the season for other hard tree fruits such as pears and Asian pears, native persimmons, and wine and table grapes. Watermelons and a few raspberries may still be around late into the season. The region's wine industry celebrates fall with wine festivals, often with dozens of wineries participating where you can get a taste of many different products and choose your favorites. Some wineries hold their own individual wine festivals with local food and music or even invite the public to help with the grape harvest for the year's winemaking.

Cool-weather vegetables, including spinach, broccoli, cabbage, and cau-

You could just as easily chop your greens and sauté them with olive oil and garlic or braise them in wine with onions. Any kind of greens can be stored this way—spinach, chard, kale, collards, mustards, turnip and beet greens, any leafy green that you cook. Just cook them as tender as you like them, cool, and freeze.

Whole tomatoes, berries, and peaches are also great candidates for freezing. Just wash tomatoes and remove the stems, lay them in a single layer on a baking sheet, and put them in the freezer, uncovered, until they are hard as billiard balls. Pile them into a plastic freezer bag and they are ready to remove, individually as needed, to brighten up soups, stews, and sauces through the winter.

The same prep works for strawberries, blueberries, and raspberries. Soft fruits such as peaches are best sliced and tossed with sugar, then frozen. The sugar helps to keep the slices separate and acts as a preservative as well. The *Ball Blue Book of Preserving* is a good reference book for freezing as well as canning, pickling, and drying.

liflower make a comeback in fall. Peppers and tomatoes, Asian greens like bok choy and tatsoi, and other types of cooking greens continue to flourish. Root vegetables abound, for cooking now or for storage—carrots, beets, turnips, potatoes, onions, garlic, and sweet potatoes, which grow extremely well here. Light, watery summer squashes give way to dense pumpkins, acorn, butternut, blue hubbard, and other winter squashes. This is the time to start stockpiling dried garlic bulbs for the winter.

A few larger turkey farms supply birds to grocers year-round, but most small farmers raise turkeys for the holiday season only. Farmers raise standard breeds such as Broad-Breasted Whites (the kind you see in the grocery store, except not factory farmed) as well as many different types of heritage turkeys that you can only get through a farmer. Some farmers require advance orders for turkeys, so ask ahead in October. STSLs (stores that source local) will have locally raised turkeys for sale as well. For hunters, there is a limited fall turkey season to bag your own Thanksgiving meal, although the main hunting season is in the spring.

Fall is still a great time for a crab feast, while watermen and anglers find most mid-Atlantic fish and shellfish abundant at this time of year as well.

Farmer Julie Bolton of Groff's Content sells a frozen Thanksgiving turkey at the Riverdale Park Farmers Market. Photo by Kristi Bahrenburg Janzen.

Winter Comfort

After the winter solstice, which falls around Christmas, marks the shortest day of the year, most of our local food needs during winter are met by those year-round foods described at the beginning of this chapter. Most produce farmers either take a break for the season or focus on growing their all-season indoor crops. There may be others, but I personally know of only one farmer, Brett Grohsgal of Even' Star Organic Farm in St. Mary's County, who grows hardy winter greens and root vegetables outdoors on open fields through snow, hail, and all kinds of winter weather. Livestock farmers must tend to their herds and flocks all year, but some poultry farmers who don't have the facilities to keep birds indoors will process and freeze the entire flock to have chicken to sell in the winter, putting out new chicks in the spring.

Winter is hunting season for ducks, geese, and deer. It's illegal to sell wild venison, so you need to know a hunter willing to share the meat from their kill. Thousands of pounds of wild venison are donated to food banks by hunters each year.

Apples are great for winter baking, as are any fruits you stored in the freezer or purchased canned from a farmer during the summer. This is the time for pork roasts and beef stews and Sunday chicken dinners. We always have friends over to watch the Super Bowl and eat chili made with grass-fed local beef and tomatoes from my freezer, topped with local dairy sour cream and Colby cheese. Trickling Springs Creamery and other dairies offer delicious eggnog, and seasonally flavored beers and spirits from local producers warm up the winter evenings.

Heirloom Varieties and Heritage Breeds

If you know only one thing about local food, it's probably heirloom tomatoes. The idea that tomatoes could taste great was not so new. Anyone who had ever grown their own knew what a fraud was being perpetrated on us by grocery store tomatoes. But very few of us knew that tomatoes did not have to be red to be ripe and juicy. Who knew about the dark-hued Cherokee Purple, or the yellow-striped Green Zebra, or bright-as-a-summer-day Sungold cherry tomatoes, before we went to a farmers market?

These lovely heirloom fruits and vegetables—tomatoes are not the only ones—are simply open-pollinated varieties, which come from seeds that can be saved and planted to get the same quality of crop, versus hybrid seeds, which have been crossbred to promote certain characteristics at the expense of being able to produce reliable seeds. Heirlooms are open-pollinated varieties that have generally not been exploited commercially, perhaps because they grow well only in certain climates, or they are too fragile to be packed and shipped. A machine can't stuff bumpy heirloom tomatoes into a cellophane sleeve.

Heritage is the same concept as heirloom, applied to livestock breeds. Similar to heirlooms, these are older breeds that may have been prized for particular characteristics in the past that became less valuable as the industrial system homogenized American preferences and prioritized volume over taste.

I've participated in some official tastings of heritage breeds of beef and turkey and have experimented on my own with lamb and pork. Turkey is by far the greatest beneficiary of the return of heritage breeds. There was really nowhere to go but up in terms of flavor and desirability from the Butterball and its ilk that had come to define Thanksgiving. Most people confess to not really being a big fan of turkey, but tradition requires that our holiday tables have a huge roasted bird in the middle. A thriving industry of turkey briners, injectors, basters, and fryers has arisen in the attempt to coax flavor out of something that is bred and raised to have none. The problem, of course, is not only the breed, which has a higher breast-to-leg meat ratio than normal, but the way the turkeys are fed and raised in confinement.

A Broad-Breasted White turkey raised free-ranging on a farm, with the opportunity to exercise its muscles and flap its wings, develops flavor that is absent from factory-farmed animals of the same breed. Heritage breeds such as Bourbon Red, Bronze, Narragansett, and Midget White take flavor to another level. The colors in the names of heritage breeds refer to feather color of the bird. Heritage birds are generally smaller than commercial turkeys, with breasts in normal proportion to the rest of the body. The breast meat is almost as dark as the legs and has a denser texture than that of commercial turkeys. In my mind, a heritage turkey is an all-dark-meat turkey, which means more moistness and flavor.

Heritage breeds of laying hens produce eggs in a range of hues, from pastel greens to vivid blues to muted and speckled browns. Light brown eggs come from brown- or red-feathered hens, and white eggs come from white-feathered hens. Almost any hen that lays blue eggs has the Araucana breed in its genes somewhere. There are also a handful of breeds known for laying very dark brown eggs.

Similar to the cardboard-ization of turkey, the Midwestern corn-fueled meat industry in the twentieth century transformed the pig from a hardy animal that could find food on its own and convert any kind of forage into a good source of protein and fat into the lean, bland, and uniform "other white meat." Local farmers have embraced breeds such as Berkshire, Tamworth, and Gloucester Old Spot, for reasons ranging from the characteristics of their meat to their qualities as farm animals in terms of handling, care, and maintenance.

The Livestock Conservancy is the best source for information about American farm animal breeds that are in danger of being lost. In many cases, creating a market value for them by eating them is the best way to ensure their survival.

Diversity in our food plants and animals builds a stronger local food system, just as diversity among people builds a stronger society. But as a final thought, I advise you not to be too concerned about becoming a breed connoisseur when you're eating. If Butterball were suddenly to start marketing Bourbon Red turkeys and every local pastured poultry farmer I know was raising only Broad-Breasted Whites (which many of them do), I would take the locally raised and pastured Broad-Breasted White every time. Ditto for a mass-marketed heirloom tomato versus a local organically grown field tomato of the most prosaic variety. Food that has been raised in an environmentally sensitive and humane way, by small-scale farmers who care, going through as few hands as possible before it gets to me, will always be worth a premium.

Creamy Potato and Kale Soup

This soup can be eaten as a hearty potage without the final step of puréeing, but the beauty of it as a creamy soup is the way it lets you slip kale in for kids or others who think they don't like its flavor. It also makes it less difficult to digest for those who have a problem with the fiber in leafy greens, something I experience with Crohn's disease and a common symptom of many other gastrointestinal disorders.

2 slices bacon or 2 tablespoons vegetable or olive oil
½ cup diced onion
3 cups chicken stock, vegetable stock, or water
4 cups diced baking potatoes (2 large potatoes)
1 cup chopped kale
½–¾ cup milk
Salt and pepper, to taste

If using bacon, cut the strips into ¼-inch pieces. In a heavy-bottomed 2-quart pot, fry the bacon, stirring frequently over medium-low heat until the fat is rendered and the pieces are crisp. Remove the bacon with a slotted spoon and drain on paper towels. Set aside.

If not using bacon, put the vegetable or olive oil in a heavy-bottomed 2-quart pot over medium heat. Add the onion to the oil or bacon fat in the pot and sauté over medium heat until it softens and begins to turn translucent, about 5 minutes. Do not let the onion brown. Add the stock or water, the potatoes, and the kale. The liquid should completely cover the vegetables. Turn the heat up to medium-high and cook until the potatoes break easily with a fork, 10–15 minutes.

Remove the pot from the heat. If you have an immersion blender, use it to purée the soup in the pot. If using a countertop blender, let the soup cool slightly before carefully puréeing it in batches in the blender. Return all the puréed soup to the pot.

Return the pot to the stove. Over medium-low heat, stir in enough milk to reach a consistency that is creamy but will still pour off a spoon, and heat through without boiling. Season with salt and pepper, garnish with the reserved bacon if you like, and serve. Serves 4–6.

3 | Farms

A trip to a pick-your-own fruit farm can be a quick initiation into the pleasures of eating local. Pulling a strawberry off a vine or a blueberry off the bush, an apple or a peach from a low-hanging tree branch, taps into our primeval gatherer instincts. We make a visceral connection to the edible landscape when we move a piece of fruit from the plant, to our hand, and finally to our mouth. For a moment, we feel powerful, like we are feeding ourselves off the land.

In our brief time on that farm, we should also get a glimpse of how hard it would be to *actually* have to feed ourselves off the land and thank our lucky stars that there are farmers whose hard work creates those farms where we can go and have our fantasy agrarian lives. We spend maybe an hour crawling along the strawberry rows on our knees or craning our necks as we walk along looking up for peaches to pull. We might work up a small sweat if the day is hot, but we walk away with the immediate gratification of beautiful fruit with amazing flavor right in our hands. We are spared the hard work it is to actually tend, nurture, and cultivate the thousands of vines, bushes, and trees required to grow enough of the grapes, berries, and tree fruits that the millions of us in greater Washington would need to survive, let alone as many as our gluttonous habits have taught us to crave for our enjoyment.

Imagine harvesting fruit all day, every day, for two or three months. Then imagine all the daily tasks and crises of the other nine or ten months that must be dealt with without knowing for sure whether the efforts will even result in a successful crop. Farmers who love farming will tell you that it may be incredibly rewarding, but it should not be romanticized—farming is hard, tiring, dirty, and all-consuming work, both physically and mentally.

Visit a farm and you begin to realize that someone has to walk or ride up and down all those rows of plants, vines, bushes, and trees over and over again, to help them fight the good fight against other plants that want their

Kristi Janzen and her kids enjoy a day in the pumpkin patch at Larriland Farm. Photo courtesy of Kristi Bahrenburg Janzen.

space and other animals that want to eat them before we can. Someone has to make sure the animals whose sacrifice will provide food for us have their own healthy food and water, as well as shelter and exercise every day throughout their lives on the farm. Someone has to stack, clean, mend, store, and move all the paraphernalia of farming from place to place endlessly— mountains of bushel crates, miles of fences, dribbling irrigation hoses, and seemingly endless piles of buckets, shovels, pitchforks, mucky boots, and muddy gloves.

Think a little longer and you might realize that someone also has to analyze the soil to determine what will grow well there or what amendments can be added to improve the soil health. Someone has to plan far in advance how much of each crop needs to be planted, which crops to plant for each season, and how to ensure a variety of products that consumers will want to buy. Someone has to plan for the seeds to be ordered from a reputable company, especially if looking for organic, non-GM (genetically modified), and heirloom varieties, or do the tedious work of saving seeds for the farm's own use.

Meat production requires even further advance planning, especially for pastured animals that tend to grow more slowly than their confined and grain-fed counterparts. Someone has to study animal genetics to decide which breeds make sense for both the farm terrain and the kind of eggs or meat the farm wants to sell. Someone has to make the deals with equipment suppliers, feed wholesalers, packaging and labeling companies, slaughterhouses and butchers, farmers market managers and restaurants. Someone has to research and file the paperwork with federal and state agencies for any number of permits, surveys, cost-shares, rebates, and other requirements that seem to multiply every year. That "someone" is a farmer, who may be the owner of the farm business or may be a permanent or temporary farm worker.

One of my family's first farm visits was to Springfield Farm in Baltimore County to buy meat back in 2005. There is no pick-your-own when you visit a farm that raises animals (although there are farms where you can choose and slaughter your own goats and sheep for religious or other reasons), but gray-bearded, denim-overalled farmer Dave Smith welcomed us in the small parking lot at the back of his house, outside the garage that had been converted to a small farm store. He encouraged me and my husband Damon to take the kids—Catie was 7, Louis was 5—on a walk around the farm to see how the animals were cared for before we made our purchases.

We wandered down the field behind the house to pastures where a few goats and a flock of white-feathered chickens destined for the dinner table were grazing. Ducks were waddling toward a pond in a dip near the woods. Back up the field, out the driveway and a little ways up the farm road we'd come in on, we found the red-feathered laying hens, clucking and scratching around a sloping field surrounding a barn-inspired henhouse. Across the farm road in another field whose purpose I didn't know—maybe it was regrowing pasture, maybe hay for the winter—we found large rabbit hutches. These bunnies, big and meaty, were also destined for dinner. Springfield Farm fit the picture in my mind's eye of a quaint, sustainable local food farm in every way. The only thing that surprised me was the above-ground pool full of splashing grandkids, in the grass between the garage (turned farm store) and the broiler pasture.

No two farms are exactly alike. I've visited dozens of different kinds of farms, and I learn something new every time. Our local farms are fairly diverse and becoming more so day by day. They vary in size, in the kinds of crops and livestock they sustain, in the way they approach their environment.

While some large farms and confined animal operations do exist in the Chesapeake region, mostly in the industrial poultry and feed sector that dominates the Eastern Shore, the majority of our farms are relatively small, averaging just 165 acres per farm in Maryland, 175 in West Virginia, and 181 in Virginia, far smaller than the national average of 434 acres. Pennsylvania farms average 130 acres. Only five small New England states have a smaller average farm size. Urban farms as small as 1 or 2 acres exist in Baltimore and DC, and many rural farms thrive on not much more. Jack and Becky Gurley own Calvert's Gift Farm, a 5-acre certified organic vegetable farm in Baltimore County. Becky once told me that they never wanted to be bigger; those 5 acres have put their kids through college.

Chalk some of the small farm size up to the population density and sprawling development of the Eastern Seaboard. The topography of rivers, hills, valleys, and the great Chesapeake Bay also creates natural breaks in our landscape that are not present in the flat midwestern grasslands. To the benefit of local consumers, farms of this size and landscape may not be able to support a family dependent on producing cheap commodity crops like corn and soybeans. But they can do quite well for farmers who want to grow high quality, nutrient-dense, flavorful vegetables and fruits on a scale compatible with the hands-on human labor required by organic and other sustainable agriculture techniques.

The US Department of Agriculture considers $1,000 in food sales the threshold for calling a tract of food-producing land a farm. That amount of revenue represents basically a hobby farm, maybe someone growing herbs or making jams from wild berries and selling them at a small farmers market. Still, nearly 75 percent of Maryland farms and 85 percent of Virginia farms *gross* less than $50,000 each year. The next most profitable 10 percent in each state gross between $50,000 and $250,000. Only 6 percent of Virginia farmers and 15 percent of Maryland farmers gross more than $250,000 a year. Once they pay for their supplies, seeds, animal feed, tools, machinery maintenance, field and market staff, and other expenses, some local farmers

Farmers at Willowsford Farm in Loudoun County, Virginia. Photo by Deborah Dramby.

can make a decent living. But a lot of farmers still have to work other jobs off the farm to make ends meet.

Although we talk a lot about small, family farms in the local food system, being small is not a virtue in and of itself, and being large doesn't necessarily mean a farm is not doing the right thing. That's why visiting farms and meeting farmers can be so valuable. When you are buying directly from a farmer—by which I also mean the extended family and staff that might be working at a market stand or CSA pickup—you have a better chance of understanding whether the food has been grown in a way you're comfortable with. You are not going to encounter a poultry factory farmer at a farmers market, but you will meet farmers who use a variety of farming techniques.

Farming Methods

"Local" is a geographic term. It does not automatically equate to small, organic, sustainable, biodynamic, humane, fair employer, or any other measure of farm practices, philosophy, or ethics other than place. You won't see a lot of food labels and certifications when you buy direct from local farmers at farmers markets or farm stands, through CSAs or buying clubs. What you should see is a willingness to talk about the farm's practices and to have consumers visit the farm within respectful parameters. This transparency

My daughter Catie and other young visitors getting to know the cattle at Clagett Farm during a farm open house. Photo by Renee Brooks Catacalos.

offers the possibility of digging deeper to evaluate other characteristics of a local farm for yourself.

The more you can educate yourself about farming methods, the more you'll be able to understand about what you hear or see from farmers. But if you don't want to get into the proverbial or literal weeds, let me give you a quick primer on a few important concepts you'll encounter:

* why some farms are Certified Organic and others that employ organic methods are not;

* what organic and pastured mean for livestock production; and

* how all of this fits into the big idea of sustainable agriculture

Organic Methods and Certification

You and I may know how to drive, understand and obey all the rules, and be the safest drivers in the world, but if we do not take the state-required test, present our documents, and pay our fee to get a driver's license, we will not be legal drivers.

A farmer, or a backyard gardener for that matter, may take classes and read everything there is to read about organic agriculture and follow the organic rules of the USDA to the letter. But unless that farmer submits required documents, has the required inspection, and pays the required fees, the farm cannot legally be called Certified Organic.

That's the basic difference between those who are Certified Organic and those who say they farm organically or use other terms related to organic methods. Farmers who choose certification feel that it's a trusted and well-recognized sign to the consumer that they take their growing methods seriously and are willing to have a third party certify that for the consumer's benefit. That's valuable to a lot of consumers who know that extra work and expense is involved in organic certification and believe that justifies paying a premium for food produced that way.

Non-labor costs for conventional farmers are mostly for continual purchasing of seeds, fertilizer, herbicides, and pesticides. Organic farmers have lower expenses for these inputs but have higher labor costs for the same yield, because they do a lot of weed and pest control mechanically or by hand, as opposed to spraying chemicals on the problems. This additional labor and care, along with the external benefits of minimal toxic residue on food and less damage to the environment, account for the added value and sometimes higher cost of organically farmed produce.

The USDA definition used for organic certification states:

> Organic is a labeling term for food or other agricultural products that have been produced using cultural, biological, and mechanical practices that support the cycling of on-farm resources, promote ecological balance, and conserve biodiversity in accordance with the USDA organic regulations. This means that organic operations must maintain or enhance soil and water quality, while also conserving wetlands, woodlands, and wildlife. Synthetic fertilizers, sewage sludge, irradiation, and genetic engineering may not be used.

There are a lot of specific rules and trade-offs that come under this general definition. For instance, "organic" does not mean the farmer is not allowed to use pesticides, herbicides, or fungicides. It means the farmer is allowed to use only pesticides, herbicides, and fungicides made from organic or naturally occurring substances. These natural substances are also toxic in some way to the offending pest, plant, or fungus and many of them must still be used carefully to avoid harm to the environment or the health of the workers applying them.

Most of the farmers using organic methods and selling directly to consumers try not to use any pesticides, herbicides, or fungicides at all. They use cultural practices such as building up healthy soil that strengthens plants' ability to fight off pests and disease, choosing native plant varieties with built-in resistance to local diseases, and planting naturally pest-repellent companion plants such as marigolds with tomatoes. They use biological practices like introducing beneficial insects to prey upon the ones they don't want. Organic farmers generally control weeds with mechanical practices, including chopping and pulling them out, tilling them under, or suppressing them with newspaper or black plastic.

Why would a farmer go to all this trouble to grow organically and not get organic certification? Cost is a factor for some. The cost to get certified can range from a few hundred dollars to several thousand depending on the size,

Farm Certifications

Certified Organic—See the definition on page 55. Check online at https://organic.ams.usda.gov/integrity/ to see the status of any farm claiming to be Certified Organic or to search for Certified Organic farms. Nearly four hundred farms and businesses are listed across Maryland and Virginia.

Certified Naturally Grown (CNG)—Based on the National Organic Program standards, this certification is administered by a peer-to-peer network of farmers. CNG is less expensive and less paperwork intensive in its efforts to better serve smaller farms growing produce or raising animals organically. Certified Naturally Grown offers a database of certified farms on its website at https://certified.naturallygrown.org/.

Certified Biodynamic—The Demeter Biodynamic Farm Standard reflects the biodynamic principle of the farm as a living organism: self-contained, self-sustaining, following the cycles of nature. Its requirements go beyond organic standards to "capture key agronomic principles not comprehensively addressed within any other agriculture certification system." The number of certified biodynamic farms in Maryland and Virginia listed at Demeter's website, www.biodynamicfood.org, could be counted on one hand, but more farms say they use biodynamic principles.

Regenerative Organic Certified—This brand new certification developed by a coalition led by the Rodale Institute, a leading organic research organi-

type, and complexity of the farm, and the certification has to be regularly renewed. The paperwork and reporting requirements can seem onerous for small farmers or not the best use they could make of their limited time and resources. Some are simply not interested in any more interactions with the government than what are absolutely required.

Some farmers reject certification because they feel that the National Organic Program's standards haven't kept up with advances in organic farming methods or have been watered down by corporate interests that market "industrial organic" produce and processed organic foods. These farmers might use terms like "beyond organic" or "ecological" or "biological" to describe their farming methods. "Biodynamic" is a holistic approach to farming that sees the farm and all its processes as an integrated, living, and regenerative organism. A farm must meet the National Organic Program standard for organic certification plus additional requirements in order to be certified Biodynamic by Demeter USA.

At the 2018 sustainable agriculture conference held by Future Harvest–

zation, aims to "facilitate widespread adoption of holistic, regenerative practices throughout agriculture. It builds on the standards set forth by USDA Organic and similar programs internationally, particularly in the areas of animal welfare and farmer and worker fairness." The principles of the certification are explained at https://rodaleinstitute.org/regenerativeorganic/.

Animal Welfare Approved (AWA)– This organization's standards require that domesticated farm animals must be able to behave naturally and be in a state of physical and psychological well-being. They are based on the concept that the way we raise our animals, the nutritional quality of the food they produce, and the impact of the farming system on the environment are all intrinsically linked. AWA approval is only awarded to family farms. State-by-state listings of approved farms and some of the places that sell their products is at https://animalwelfareapproved.us/farms/.

*Certified Humane–*This organization's mission is to improve the lives of farm animals from birth to slaughter, with standards that cover living conditions, ability to exhibit natural behaviors, food, and slaughter methods. The Certified Humane label is more often on large supermarket brands than small farm labels. See a list of producers at https://certifiedhumane.org/whos-certified/ and a list of stores and restaurants that carry Certified Humane meats at https://certifiedhumane.org/take-action-for-farm-animals/shop-2/.

CASA (Chesapeake Alliance for Sustainable Agriculture), keynote speaker Gabe Brown, a cattle rancher from North Dakota and renowned expert on building healthy grazing soils, spoke about regenerative agriculture, which many farmers are now learning more about. Brown told the crowd that soils get depleted no matter what. "Sustainable is not good enough. Why sustain a depleted resource? We have to be regenerating our soils."

Meat—Organic, Pastured, and Other Methods

Livestock farmers have a different relationship with organic certification. Meat and eggs can be Certified Organic provided the animals were fed a Certified Organic diet free of GMOs (genetically modified organisms), antibiotics, and hormones, whether that diet consists of grains or grass. For meat, the slaughter facility must also be Certified Organic. The lack of Certified Organic slaughterhouse capacity is an obstacle to organic labeling for small farmers of beef, goat, and lamb, which must be processed in a USDA-approved facility. Farms that sell below a certain threshold of poultry are permitted to slaughter the chickens on-farm, so if the farm and feed are Certified Organic, the chickens can be, too.

For many local farmers and local eaters, whether the animals have been raised on pasture can be more important than whether the meat is certified organic, although ideally the pasture itself would be organic or as close to it as possible. Few local farmers use the term "free-range," which the USDA defines for poultry as the requirement that birds have *access* to the outdoors. This could mean an open door at the far end of a long chicken warehouse filled with thousands of chickens, as long as they are not confined to cages. It is no guarantee that the birds actually ever set foot on grass.

While the USDA does not have an official definition for "pastured," the American Pastured Poultry Producers Association describes it this way:

> Pastured poultry relies on raising chickens directly on green pasture. The model has been developed over the last twenty years and allows the birds to receive a significant amount of pasture forage as feed. The birds are kept on fresh pasture, which allows the birds to be raised in a cleaner, healthier environment. Pastured poultry is raised the old-fashioned way; on fresh green pasture and wholesome grain.

Pastured poultry are raised in open-air fields where they can eat grass and other greens and peck the ground for bugs, worms, and grubs in addition to grain. The added protein they pick up from these insects is what leads to

Additional Local Food Directories

Amazing Grazing
https://www.futureharvestcasa
.org/resources/amazing-grazing
-directory

Find farms in Delaware, Maryland, Virginia, and West Virginia that raise grass-fed and pastured meat, dairy, and poultry for sale directly to consumers.

DC Greens Food Access Resources
http://dcgreens.org/food-access
-resources/

Find DC farmers markets, including those that redeem SNAP (Supplemental Nutrition Assistance Program), Produce Plus, and other food benefits, plus food access sites such as community gardens, emergency food, and healthy corner stores by ward.

Maryland Farmers Market Association
http://www.marylandfma.org/

This database can filter farmers markets across Maryland by location, day of the week, and the types of food and nutrition benefit programs accepted.

Virginia Market Maker
https://va.foodmarketmaker.com/

Search the database for mapped links to a variety of farms, farmers markets, and food businesses, which can be filtered for dozens of criteria, including kosher and halal.

Washington Post–Find a CSA Interactive Map
https://www.washingtonpost.com
/graphics/food/csa-community
-supported-agriculture-interactive
-map/?tid=a_inl

This interactive map of farms offering Community Supported Agriculture (CSA) shares lets you search by pick-up locations offered in DC, Maryland, Virginia, and West Virginia.

Washington Post–Farmers Markets in the Washington Area
https://www.washingtonpost.com
/graphics/food/dc-farmers-markets
-interactive-map/

This interactive map of nearly 200 farmers markets across DC, Maryland, and Virginia lets you search by market day and benefits accepted, as well as by geographic location.

eggs with naturally higher levels of omega-3 fatty acids and brilliant yellow-colored yolks. Pastured birds also benefit from the exercise and freedom to move that comes with their outdoor lifestyle, which develops their muscles and deepens the flavor of the meat.

Ruminants—sheep, goats, cattle, bison, and water buffalo (yes, local water buffalo!)—possess digestive systems that have evolved to break down grasses and fibrous plants that other mammals can't eat. These foods are their natural "salad bar," as described by Virginia farmer Joel Salatin, who popularized among small-scale farmers the practice of rotational grazing, or moving animals to fresh pasture frequently and systematically. While ruminants can digest small quantities of grain and, in fact, will eat it happily as if it were candy, grain alters their gut chemistry. Their gut bacteria is calibrated to work on grasses and forage. Too much grain can cause damage to their digestive systems. Ruminants that eat nothing but pasture grasses and grass hays up until slaughter can be called 100 percent grass-fed or grass-finished. Those that have grazed most of their lives but are given grain to fatten up for a short period prior to slaughter are called grass-fed and grain-finished.

Some experts, including animal scientist and livestock behavior specialist Temple Grandin, maintain that a certain ration of grain in a well-managed environment can also offer health benefits without major digestive difficulties. Feeding cattle grain allows them to fatten up to slaughter weight in as few as eighteen months, while grass-fed cattle can take as long as twenty-four to thirty months. However, some studies have shown that cattle eating only grass produce 20 percent less methane (a greenhouse gas) than those that are fed grain.

As omnivores, pigs have always been one of the most valuable of all farm animals. Pigs that are allowed to forage for food are called pastured. They can be turned loose both in fields and in wooded land where you can't graze any other animals, and they will find all kinds of things to eat, including insects and larvae, nuts and fruit that have fallen from trees, and roots and tubers that they dig up. In the process, they also help turn and aerate the soil of the forest floor so it becomes even more productive. They are also living garbage disposals for kitchen scraps, the apple residue from cider pressing, spent grains from beer brewing, and culls from the vegetable harvest.

Just keep in mind that "organic" does not mean "grass-fed" or "pastured," nor is the reverse true. Putting animals on good, healthy pasture or forage not only provides them with the proper nutritious food they have evolved to eat, it also allows them to move around and find their food in the ways they were meant to. The National Organic Program is working on new rules to better address livestock and poultry living conditions and handling prior to slaughter. These and other welfare certifications may be more important when you are buying meat in stores from medium to large producers. For direct purchases from small local farmers, the information you can get from

Berkshire pigs at Cabin Creek Heritage Farm in Upper Marlboro, Maryland, root and forage in the farm's woodlands year-round. Photo by Louis Catacalos.

talking to them and, if possible, visiting their farms, should tell you what you need to know.

Sustainable Agriculture

The concept of sustainability is built into conversations about local food systems, but it's not always clear exactly what it means. Farms may say they grow food or raise animals in a sustainable manner. Organizations say they support sustainable agriculture or sustainable farming. We want to build a sustainable local food system. "Sustainable" describes the way we grow food, as well as the impact the production of the food and the operations of a farm or food business have on the people and places around them.

The USDA's official definition of sustainability resides, ironically, on the website of the National Agricultural Library's Alternative Farming Systems Information Center (AFSIC). A document on sustainable agriculture terms and definitions, last updated in 2007, says, "Although certainly not mainstream at this point, sustainable agriculture is now being addressed by the agricultural community in significant ways." Odd that the idea of sustainability, which seems like a natural survival mechanism for any species, would

CSA participants can pick and choose their favorite peppers at Clagett Farm in Upper Marlboro, Maryland. Photo by Renee Brooks Catacalos.

ever *not* be mainstream or that it would be an *alternative* farming system, but this is where the takeover by the industrial food system has landed us.

The AFSIC page goes on to refer to the 1990 Farm Bill:

The term sustainable agriculture means an integrated system of plant and animal production practices having a site-specific application that will, over the long term:

* satisfy human food and fiber needs;
* enhance environmental quality and the natural resource base upon which the agricultural economy depends;
* make the most efficient use of nonrenewable resources and on-farm resources and integrate, where appropriate, natural biological cycles and controls;
* sustain the economic viability of farm operations; and
* enhance the quality of life for farmers and society as a whole.

Another branch of the USDA, called Sustainable Agriculture Research and

Education (SARE) distills this down to what it calls the 3 Pillars of Sustainability:

1. Profit over the long term

2. Stewardship of our nation's land, air and water

3. Quality of life for farmers, ranchers and their communities

These concepts are often expressed in business terms as the "triple bottom line"—the goal of sustaining people, planet, and profits. Sustainability encompasses not just the farming practices and outcomes but also the impact of a farm's business and social practices. This is where we remind ourselves that farming is a career, just like whatever career we pursue in order to make the money we spend on food from local farms. Those farmers are also trying to make the money to buy the products and services they need from others in our local community. Farm organizations pay workers, who are trying to make an honest living.

Nobody likes to get ripped off or be disrespected, whether they are the buyer or the seller or the owner or the worker. When people feel that they are getting the short end of the stick, eventually they find something else to do or someone else to do business with. For the local food system to be sustainable, each of us who participates has to be educated enough about what the others are doing to afford them the respect and financial consideration they deserve for the role they play.

It helps to think of sustainability as a continuum, so that even if we don't have a choice that we feel meets 100 percent of our personal priorities, we can decide which options are better than others. It helps us to recognize that farmers are people who have to make choices and compromises just as we do. A local fruit farm may bring the most flavorful, in-season fruit to market less than a day after it's picked, pay its seasonal farm workers well, and contribute to the local economy. But a successful crop may require the application of a chemical fungicide to combat diseases that thrive in humidity. A Certified Organic fruit farm on the West Coast uses fossil fuels to ship its fruit across the country and must pick the fruit before it's ripe in order to survive the shipping but keeps chemicals out of the environment. Each would be a sustainable choice in different ways, but neither is perfect.

As we are all individuals and have life experiences that affect the priorities we hold most dear, the holistic nature of defining sustainability allows us each to make choices that come closest to fulfilling our highest priorities as much as possible within our resources. We get back to the idea of taking control over our choices rather than choosing based simply on this prescribed label or that. To make the choices, we must have information and we must actually think about what we grow, buy, and eat.

Who Farms

Feeding people today is big business. In the United States overall, farms produce about 1 percent of the country's GDP, and the total agriculture, food, and related industries sector contributes about 5.5 percent. Only 1.4 percent of the labor force is directly employed in farming, but more than 11 percent is involved across the agriculture, food, and related industries, including restaurants. More than 14 percent of the US manufacturing workforce is involved in some aspect of food manufacturing, including meat and poultry processing, beverage manufacturing, bakeries, and other processed food fabrication.

Agriculture is the largest commercial sector in both Maryland and Virginia, reflecting the farming legacy of these states. Statistics from the 2012 Census of Agriculture showed that 98 percent of the nearly 12,300 farms in Maryland and 96 percent of the more than 43,000 farms in Virginia were operated by white farmers.

In both states, about 32 percent of all farmers were women, which tracked with the national average and was slightly lower than the corresponding number from the 2007 census. However, the USDA's Local Food Marketing Practices Survey, first conducted in 2015 to track characteristics of farms that sell through direct local channels, found that 38 percent of these farms are operated by women.

Farming probably evolved from the gathering done by women in early human cultures, while the men hunted. Over time, farming in America became associated with men, especially as it came to involve ranching and livestock, the large grain farms and orchards that pushed European settlements west across the continent, and the commodity plantations and farms of the South. But farmers' wives were often the ones who managed the kitchen garden, with the vegetables and fruits that were eaten on the farmers' tables. The women cooked, canned and preserved produce, meats, and fish, made cheese and butter, brewed beer, and tended the poultry for eggs and meat. Women

The Limits of Labels

Nick Maravell raises 100 percent grass-fed beef on his farm in Buck-eystown, Maryland, grazing them on his Certified Organic farm, from which he also sells Certified Organic hay and grain to other farmers. Nick has been farming organically since 1979 and served on the National Organic Standards Board from 2011 to 2016. He is considered one of the commercial organic farming pioneers in our area. But the beef from Nick's Organic Farm cannot be labeled Certified Organic because there is no slaughterhouse in the mid-Atlantic that is certified to handle organic livestock. How would that knowledge affect your choice between certified organic beef from the Midwest and Nick's local, organically raised beef slaughtered in a facility that also processes nonorganic animals?

Joan and Drew Norman's One Straw Farm was the largest Certified Organic vegetable farm in Maryland until 2010, when they voluntarily, but not without a fight, gave up their organic certification. They continue to farm using organic methods, as they have since 1983, but they felt that the National Organic Program (NOP) disallowing a new cornstarch-based, biodegradable mulch used for weed control was a failure to keep up with technology and with the larger issues of environmental sustainability. The mulch could be left on the fields to compost between seasons, whereas the NOP-approved black plastic required running a tractor across their 172-acre farm and sending four dumpsters full of plastic to the landfill every fall. In their statement to the NOP the Normans said, "It would be irresponsible of us as farmers interested and concerned about our environment to continue to use plastic just to save our certification."

are taking on larger roles in all sectors of modern American agriculture, but there is a larger increase in women farming within local food systems, where farmers of any gender who want to practice agriculture on a human scale and interact directly with those they feed can find a home.

Farms operated by African Americans are few and slowly decreasing in both states. The history of black farmers in Maryland and Virginia follows the larger story of racial bias that almost wiped out black farmers in the twentieth century. In 1920, more than half of blacks in America lived on farms, compared to about 25 percent of white Americans, and blacks represented 14 percent of all the nation's farmers. Many left the segregated South to pursue non-farming work in other parts of the country, some wanting to escape the stigma carried by the history of forced field work through enslavement and sharecropping. Those who did want to keep farming faced systemic racism in the USDA that excluded black farmers from the subsidy and loan programs that helped white farmers get through difficult times and scale up in the postwar era. A class-action lawsuit against the USDA settled in 1999 provided some compensation to thousands of black farmers, but by then many had lost their farms through foreclosures and other financial disasters. Today, African Americans make up barely 1 percent of farmers nationwide, and the land black farming families have lost may never be regained.

However, a new focus on food security and food equity as a critical issue to minority, immigrant, and low-income communities is bringing young African American farmers, along with immigrants from African and Caribbean nations, back to farming. Many of these farmers are practicing urban agriculture in underserved communities, but rural farming is also an important connection to cultural roots, as well as a necessity for producing large-enough volumes of food to make a difference. Denzel Mitchell of Five Seeds Farm began with small plots in Baltimore City but soon added a 5-acre plot in Baltimore County. Gail Taylor operates Three Part Harmony Farm on a 2-acre plot in DC's Brookland neighborhood but ensures variety for her customers through collaboration with rural farmers.

These "return generation" farmers, as Taylor styles her cohort, often did not have any direct farming experience growing up but felt a connection to the historic farming culture and traditions of Africans and their descendants in America. They have shaken off the slavery-tinged stigma of farming and embraced the independence and self-reliance that come from owning the source of your food and nourishment. Aleya Fraser and Blain Snipstal are co-owners of Black Dirt Farm near Easton on Maryland's Eastern Shore. The land they lease is historically part of the plantation where Harriet Tubman once lived, escaped, and returned to, in order to free dozens of others. Together with urban farmers in Baltimore and DC, they collaborate as the Black Dirt Farm Collective to honor and explore the black agrarian experience and to build "community, power and infrastructure" in black communities through farming and food.

There are still very few black farmers at local farmers markets, but many are forging new paths to consumers. Black Dirt Farm has partnered with Baltimore's Black Church Food Security Network to provide produce for church farmers markets. Xavier Brown of Soilful City in DC paid community gardeners in the city to help grow the heirloom fish peppers for Soilful's Pippin Sauce. In public discussions at agriculture and food systems conferences,

Farmer Rosa Linares sells Central American vegetables at the Crossroads Farmers Market. Photo by Molly M. Peterson.

young farmers of color are unapologetic in their desire to create their own local networks that minimize interaction with the mainstream local food system, which has been dominated by white farmers and consumers and has not been a welcoming environment for some farmers of color.

The number of Hispanic or Latino farmers—owners of their own farm businesses, not farm laborers—in the mid-Atlantic is small but growing and in Maryland has surpassed the paltry number of black farmers. Syracuse researcher Laura-Anne Minkoff-Zern has spent significant time interviewing Hispanic and Latino farmers in various areas of the country, including Virginia's Northern Neck, where some thirty extended families of mainly Mexican immigrants who came to the country as legal migrant workers in the berry fields have started transitioning into farming for themselves. She says these farmers today are "dealing with some of the exact same problems [as black farmers did] in terms of structural racism in agriculture."

As white farmers get older and retire, land is becoming available; former farm laborers are able to buy or rent this land to farm for themselves. Even for the farmers who have legal documentation, their rates of engagement with USDA or state extension officials are very low. One reason for this, not the only one but an important one, is the language barrier. According to Minkoff-Zern's research:

A local USDA staff member told us that there must be 10% participation in USDA programs in the region for bilingual forms to be made available. However, it is unlikely there will ever be more than 10% participation if the paperwork is not made available in Spanish in the first place. This catch-22 represents a structural problem within the USDA, which aggravates the already tenuous history of USDA.

This lack of engagement also results in likely underreporting of the numbers of Hispanic and Latino farmers in the area. Gabrielle Rovegno has worked with immigrant farmers in Maryland and Virginia through the Crossroads Farmers Market and the development of her own farming business in the Northern Neck. She has written:

The 2012 U.S. Census for Agriculture reports 14 principal farm operators of Spanish, Hispanic or Latino origin for Westmoreland County. The Westmoreland County's Extension agent can name 14 principal farm operators of Spanish, Hispanic or Latino origin farming in 500 acres of Montross, VA, let alone all of Westmoreland County. It is no surprise the numbers don't reflect the reality given the informal nature of these businesses and documentation of the farmers.

Nevertheless, these farmers are growing and selling diversified crops—including herbs such as *chipilin* that are unfamiliar to most Americans but essential to Hispanic and Latino communities—at farmers markets and to international grocery stores, carving out a place for themselves in the region's agricultural landscape.

Farms That Look Different

Springfield Farm, lovingly maintained over many generations, tapped into my storybook visions of what a farm should look like. But not everyone grew up reading books about farms or hearing anything about farms. When Margaret Morgan-Hubbard began ECO City Farms in Prince George's County in 2010, one of her goals was to show what a farm looks like to kids living inside the Capital Beltway who may not have had any concept of farming or food production at all. Urban gardening movements have begun to help kids understand that food actually comes from the ground and learn what parts of plants are edible, showing them that a carrot comes from under the ground, strawberries hide under clusters of leaves, Brussels sprouts grow like little knots on the plant stalk, and asparagus comes straight up out of the ground with no adornment, just like it looks once it is cut.

Urban farms such as ECO City Farms, Real Food Farm in Baltimore, Common Good City Farm in DC, and others take the next step to show kids and adults how food is grown in volume and how farming, even in the city, can be a source of economic development for communities. Urban farms are different from traditional rural farms in several ways, not the least of which is usually their size. Although they may be very small, they tend to employ intensive planting techniques that coax a lot of production out of the available area but also strengthen and renew urban soils organically.

Urban farms often use a combination of open fields and plastic-sided structures called hoop houses or high tunnels. Unlike greenhouses, which are permanent structures with glass walls to magnify heat, hoop houses are considered temporary structures, which allows them to be exempted from certain permitting requirements that would otherwise be an obstacle to urban farms. The plastic sides mean they can be used year-round, with the sides rolled up or removed completely in the summer for cooling and ventilation, and with the sides down to hold in enough heat to prevent plants from freezing in the winter.

Introducing productive green space to an urban neighborhood can help mitigate both the rainwater runoff and heat island effects of extensively paved spaces. Raised garden beds filled with new soil can be installed on top of pavement or existing soil to avoid growing food in soils that have been contaminated with construction materials and other pollutants. Other urban agriculture projects plant directly in the existing soil and, through the addition of organic compost and other amendments, are cleaning up and revitalizing urban soils over time. Just as often, they are turning nonproductive areas, such as vacant lots, parks that are too small to be useful for recreation, or the vast flat spaces of rooftops, into food-producing oases. When city dwellers can walk or bike down the street to buy veggies or honey or even eggs from the neighborhood farm, you get food that is truly emission-free from farm to table.

ECO City Farms and Common Good City Farm are right in the middle of neighborhoods where people can actually see them and interact. Some

Common Good City Farm in Washington, DC, grows food in the
shadow of apartments and rowhouses, with community participation.
Photo courtesy of Common Good City Farm.

urban farms are not as visible but are nevertheless shortening the distance between farm and table. "We've gotten even more local," Ellen Gray told me, about how their sourcing has changed at Equinox restaurant in recent years. "I'm buying lettuce from kids in their 20s who grow it on a rooftop in DC, incredibly beautiful produce, grown on top of a government building, a mile from the restaurant."

The way farms are owned and managed varies as well. Urban farms are much more likely to be nonprofit organizations or entrepreneurial ventures than they are to be owned by members of one family. Urban farms generally don't involve land ownership or living on the farm. But they are the exceptions to the rule. Even as we decry the rise of corporate or industrial agriculture, I was surprised to discover that 99 percent of American farms, including many very, very large farms, are actually family farms.

A farmer who owns and lives on the farmland derives economic benefits in terms of equity and reduced housing costs that business partners or the staff of a nonprofit farm may not be able to enjoy. Family farmers also feel a connection to their family's history and a special sense of pride in the stewardship of the land and the legacy they'd like to pass on to their children. Family ownership is not a guarantee of business success, but families run by second, third, or subsequent generations, who chose to continue farming because they love it, certainly can claim an advantage.

Rural farms hooked into the local food system can also have unique ownership structures. Frederick's Common Market grocery co-op operates its own farm in Boonsboro, Maryland, employing two people to grow produce for the store. Clagett Farm in Upper Marlboro, Maryland, is owned by the Chesapeake Bay Foundation and employs several farmers and educators. Arcadia Farm on Woodlawn Estate in Alexandria is a nonprofit that operates

Be a Good Guest

Even one single farm visit will help give you context for the information and food claims that come at you from all sides. The more farms you can visit, the better equipped you will be to evaluate those claims and choose food that meets your requirements for sustainability.

Whatever form your farm visit takes, be sure to contact the farm first to check their public hours, tour times, or procedure for visiting. Never show up at a farm outside its posted hours for public access. You wouldn't show up out of the blue at a commercial bakery or a machine shop and expect to be allowed in to look around. Nor would you probably be welcomed if you walked into a stranger's backyard to see their garden or play with their family dogs without an invitation. A farm is a place of work and safety-regulated food production and also, in most cases, someone's home.

Check a farm's policy on bringing small children or pets before visiting. Be careful not to wander off on a farm to any areas that farm staff has not cleared for public access. And be sure to dress appropriately for farm tours or working in fields. Sturdy, closed shoes are usually a good idea, and depending on the weather and the crops you might be walking through or even working in, long pants could also be warranted for protection against insects such as ticks and plants like poison ivy.

Alcohol tasting rooms on farms are strictly regulated and must abide by certain laws regarding outside food and beverage consumed on the premises. Know what you are allowed to bring and how many people the tasting room can accommodate before you go. And remember, a tasting room is not a bar. It's there so you can sample what's on offer and purchase what you like to take home and enjoy later.

through a partnership with the National Trust for Historic Preservation. Willowsford Farm is an amenity of the Willowsford master-planned community in Loudoun County, Virginia.

A farm owned by a business or a nonprofit may be able to provide its farm staff with a reliable salary and benefits that independent farmers could not. It's difficult and expensive for an aspiring farmer to purchase land in the Chesapeake region. Farming someone else's land or working for a small farm business lets these beginning farmers learn whether it's truly the lifestyle for them, while they save and decide whether to invest in their own land.

The "family farm" claim has value, but it may not be the most illuminating characteristic when considering how a farm fits into the local sustainable food system. Jim Perdue is of the third generation of his family to lead Perdue Farms, "the family-owned parent company of Perdue Foods and Perdue AgriBusiness," based in Salisbury, Maryland. His forebears did begin as chicken farmers, but Perdue Farms is not a farm operator today. The agricultural enterprises that grow chickens under contract for Perdue and other poultry conglomerates are, in most cases, family businesses. But you will never see a chicken as you drive by these "farms," which are actually clusters of warehouses confining as many as fifty thousand birds each for the six weeks it takes to grow them to slaughter size under highly controlled indoor conditions.

The growth of the local food system can offer these farm families other options for staying on their land and helping to feed their neighbors in a more environmentally sustainable and humane way. Look up the story of Carole Morison, featured in the movie *Food, Inc.*, who threw in the towel on industrial chicken farming for Perdue. She has transitioned her Bird's Eye View Farm to become the first Certified Humane egg operation on the Eastern Shore. Now, six hundred laying hens roam outdoors and shelter in a converted chicken house that used to hold more than fifty thousand broilers. The Virginia farmers who raise chickens for Shenandoah Valley Organics have reduced the scale of their chicken houses so they can provide a living environment for the birds that qualifies as Certified Organic and Certified Humane. They also operate as partners of the company that sells the birds, rather than contract growers, which gives them more control over their own businesses and financial sustainability.

Indoor farming of vegetables has greatly expanded the availability of locally grown lettuces and other leafy greens, tomatoes, cucumbers, herbs, and some berries. Greenhouse growing can be done in soil just like it would be outdoors or using hydroponics, a system of feeding plant roots with liquid nutrients instead of planting in soil. The recent decision to allow organic certification of hydroponic farms was controversial, as many adherents of organic agriculture believe the point is to nourish people through the transfer of nutrients from healthy soil to the plants that we eat.

Some hydroponic growers such as Purcellville, Virginia's, Endless Summer Harvest sell mainly at farmers markets. Mock's Greenhouse, in Berkeley Springs, West Virginia, has been producing since 2005 in wholesale quantities, selling to local distributors and grocery stores including Whole Foods and Wegmans. BrightFarms is based in New York but operates a hydroponic farm in Culpeper, Virginia, that grows exclusively for the Giant/Martin's/Peapod stores.

A diversity of farm sizes and types can play a role in making more local food choices available to us all.

Greek-style Moussaka

It's misleading to talk about "farm-to-table" cuisine. Farm-to-table is a way of cooking, relying on locally sourced and mostly seasonal ingredients, that can support any cuisine. Sometimes the ingredients for particular types of cuisines may not be readily available locally, but remember, every little bit counts. I can make my mother's southern homestyle fried chicken with local poultry and her macaroni and cheese with local cheddar cheese, milk, and eggs, but the macaroni is going to come from the grocery store. Likewise, I can make all sorts of taco and tamale fillings from local ingredients, but I buy masa harina or tortillas from the store because there are important differences in the kind of corn used and the process for preparing it.

I learned how to make this moussaka from my father-in-law, a first-generation Greek American cook and restaurateur. Over the years, I've found that Greek and Turkish dishes lend themselves very easily to local sourcing. In this recipe, I generally use regular store-bought flour for a smooth béchamel sauce, but Daisy pastry flour, which is milled from locally grown wheat, should work just as well. I have yet to find a local cheese that is a good substitute for Parmesan, but everything else, save the pepper and nutmeg, can be found right here in our own backyard.

4 tablespoons butter or margarine
1 pound ground beef or lamb
2 medium onions, chopped

(continued)

2 tablespoons parsley, chopped
2-3 large ripe tomatoes, diced
¼ cup good red wine
1 teaspoon coarse salt
Fresh ground pepper, to taste
1 large eggplant
Olive oil or nonstick spray
6 tablespoons butter
4 tablespoons flour
2 cups warm milk
2 eggs, beaten
½ cup grated Parmesan or Romano cheese
¼ teaspoon nutmeg

Preheat the oven to 400°F.

Heat a large skillet over medium-high heat, add the butter or margarine, and brown the ground beef or lamb with the chopped onions. Add the parsley, tomatoes, wine, salt, and pepper and lower heat to medium-low. Simmer uncovered for 30 minutes.

While the meat is simmering, strip off the eggplant skin with a vegetable peeler, then slice the eggplant lengthwise into ½-inch slices. You should have 8-10 slices. Lay the eggplant slices out on two baking sheets and lightly coat each side of the slices with a few drops of olive oil or cooking spray. Put the sheets in the oven and monitor the eggplant as it bakes, turning the slices once or twice until they are soft but not falling apart. This should take about 5-8 minutes on each side.

Lower the oven to 350°F. Spray a deep 8-inch square casserole dish with nonstick spray. Place a layer of eggplant slices on the bottom of the casserole dish and sprinkle with salt. Spread half the meat filling on top. Add another layer of eggplant with a sprinkling of salt. Cover with the remaining meat filling, and finish with a final layer of eggplant. Set aside while you make the cheese soufflé topping.

In a heavy saucepan, melt the butter over medium heat. Whisk in the flour until smooth. Slowly pour in the warm milk, whisking to blend. Continue cooking and whisking over medium heat until the mixture thickens, 5-10 minutes. Remove from heat. Whisk in the beaten eggs thoroughly, then add the cheese and nutmeg. Pour this mixture over the casserole, covering the entire surface, but be careful not to overfill.

Bake 35-45 minutes, until the topping has puffed up and browned. Remove from oven and let stand at least 30 minutes before serving. It is excellent made a day ahead and reheated. Serves 4-6.

4 | Waters

Despite its impressive size and the frequency with which it's invoked to describe this region, the disconnect between the Chesapeake Bay and the majority of people living in its watershed has never been greater. For most of us, the water is out of sight and out of mind. We rarely think about how the cars we drive, the lawn we take care of, the waste we dispose of, and the food we choose affect the body of water that is truly the beating heart of our region.

Even with all its challenges, the Chesapeake Bay is still the most biologically diverse and productive estuary in our country. The future sustainability of our local waters, including rivers, inlets, marshlands, and the Atlantic coast, will depend partly on changes in what we put into the Bay—air pollution, fertilizer and manure runoff from fields, trash and sediment in runoff from our concrete jungles. But it will also depend on a more balanced approach to what we take out of the Bay.

We have harvested the "big three"—blue crabs, oysters, and rockfish—to near extinction, while largely overlooking the majority of the edible species available in our local waters. That's starting to change.

Active monitoring and management of fisheries has helped these three premium species stabilize and begin to rebound from long years of decline in populations and catches. Aquaculture—the "farming" of clams, oysters, and some species of fish—is proving to be a profitable and environmentally friendly alternative to depleting the wild stocks of these species. Invasive species such as cownose rays and blue catfish are being aggressively harvested and marketed for their culinary appeal, to keep their numbers from overwhelming native species. Greater consumer awareness of the varieties of local fish and seafood and the willingness to vary our choices beyond the "big three" can go a long way toward ensuring increasing abundance from the Bay.

I grew up surrounded by crab lovers but also by lovers of the many vari-

Rockfish and perch on ice. Photo courtesy of Chesapeake's Bounty.

eties of small, somewhat bony fish that inhabit the Chesapeake. My mother fried fish at least once or twice a week when I was growing up. These were local fish like porgies and croakers and spot, more often than not from one of her brothers' fishing expeditions to Deal Island or the mouth of the Chesapeake. They would come back with coolers full of fish, dozens of them, a couple of pounds each, just the right size for an individual serving when fried.

My mother can easily tell the difference between yellow perch and ocean perch or croakers and butterfish. I like eating them all, but haven't yet developed her level of discernment of which species is which once they are cooked. But one fish I love and can easily identify is bluefish. I acquired a taste for bluefish (not to be confused with blue catfish) during my two years in Istanbul in the late 1980s and was surprised to find when I returned to Maryland that it's a common local fish as well. Apparently my family considers it too oily. In fact, it is an oily fish with an assertive flavor and not suited for frying, which was always the go-to preparation at home. But it's fantastic on the grill, seasoned with herbs, salt, and pepper—the way it's usually prepared alongside the banks of the Bosphorus—and it's also a good candidate for the smoker. Along with herring and Atlantic mackerel, bluefish is also a great local source of healthy omega-3 fatty acids.

But enough of my fish tales. Let's talk about the rockfish, called striped bass by folks outside the Chesapeake Bay, a tasty firm-fleshed fish, similar to red snapper or halibut. Whole rockfish for sale in stores can weigh several pounds, enough to serve whole as an impressive main dish. Rockfish also yield thick, meaty fillets, making them versatile for use in restaurants and

Eating the Invaders

Invasive species can be damaging to an ecosystem and are usually very difficult to eradicate. With edible invaders, some say, if you can't beat them, eat them!

The blue catfish is a freshwater fish introduced to tributary rivers in the 1970s as a sport fish. It is an aggressive predator that quickly became more populous in the Bay's tributaries than the native channel catfish, eating anything in its way, including important native species such as menhaden, shad, and blue crabs. The nonprofit Wide Net Project educates the public about the threat blue catfish pose to the Bay, as well as how delicious it is as a food fish. Not to be confused with the dense and oily (in a good way) bluefish, blue catfish is a flaky white fish that can be fried, baked, or roasted like native catfish.

One of the best methods of controlling wild blue catfish, an invasive species that preys on native Bay denizens, is by eating it in delicious preparations like crispy blue catfish with lemon. Photo by Jenny Holm / Wide Net Project.

The Wide Net Project promotes commercial sales of blue catfish through its distribution partner, seafood wholesaler J. J. McDonnell, resulting in blue catfish on menus across the region and across the country. Blue catfish fillets are available to buy locally at MOM's Organic Market stores and other retailers, and through 4P Foods' subscription service. The Wide Net Project also raises funds to donate blue catfish to local hunger relief programs like Miriam's Kitchen.

Chesapeake cownose ray is another destructive invasive species that preys on the Bay's oysters. Restaurants offer the occasional ray or skate wing dishes, but the campaign to "save the bay, eat a ray" didn't take off with quite the impact the blue catfish promotion has achieved. Luckily, new studies are suggesting that the cownose ray's impact on the oyster population is not as significant as once thought.

easy for those who don't like dealing with bones. The flavor is mild but appealing, and it pairs well with lots of sauces and sides. It's most often roasted or seared.

Rockfish is also a popular sport fish all along the Atlantic Coast from Maine to North Carolina, but nowhere more than in the Chesapeake Bay. It's been the Maryland state fish since 1965 and is the most important commercial and recreational fish Bay-wide. The state record for a rockfish caught in Maryland is more than 67 pounds, set by an angler in 1995. The Bay's shellfish harvests are actually more lucrative, but the catch value of rockfish has been between $11 million and $15 million annually since 2011. Adding what's spent on boats, charters, fishing gear, travel, and other related expenses, rockfish attract about $500 million to the local economy annually.

The rockfish was the first of the big three Chesapeake Bay species to successfully reverse its decline. After record-high catches of nearly fifteen million pounds in 1973, the rockfish haul from the Bay had dwindled to less than two million pounds just ten years later. This decline was blamed on overfishing compounded by the generally poor state of the water in the Bay, which is the principal spawning grounds for nearly 90 percent of the Atlantic striped bass population.

In 1985, Maryland and Delaware halted fishing of rockfish. Virginia joined the moratorium in 1989. In 1990, the fishery reopened with strict catch limits, and by 1995 the rockfish fishery was declared to be fully restored. Controls against overfishing remain in place, but in the last ten years, the rockfish has become threatened by two new forces that may be linked.

In 2005, fisheries officials began to report the occurrence of a bacterial infection called mycobacteriosis in some rockfish caught in the Bay. While the bacteria do not appear to pose a threat to humans consuming fresh rockfish that has been properly stored and cooked, it could be a threat to the stability of the rockfish stock. Scientists are not yet sure whether the infection is killing off rockfish in significant numbers, but they have launched various studies to determine the connections between the rising incidence of the infection and the water quality in the Bay.

The second recent threat has come from the overfishing of the rockfish's most abundant prey, a small oily fish called menhaden. Along with oysters, menhaden have been an integral part of the filtration system of the Chesapeake Bay and waters all along the Atlantic coast for millennia. Menhaden were probably the fish swimming so thickly that Captain John Smith wrote of trying to scoop them up with a frying pan as he maneuvered his boat into

Chesapeake Bay. Menhaden were still running in schools said to be dozens of miles long in the open waters of the Atlantic in the nineteenth and early twentieth centuries.

While they are not a good eating fish for humans, menhaden are the preferred feeder fish for most of the larger edible fish in the Bay and the Atlantic, with rockfish near the very top of that food chain. Some observers think rockfish are becoming malnourished by a lack of sufficient menhaden, which makes the rockfish more vulnerable to mycobacteriosis. Menhaden themselves feed on phytoplankton, the source of the suffocating algae blooms that create oxygen-deprived dead zones in the Bay. The declining population of menhaden, the primary consumer of phytoplankton, contributes to the spread of these algae blooms that kill the aquatic plants necessary for many of the Bay's creatures to survive.

Why are the menhaden overfished if we don't eat them? It turns out we do, circuitously. Menhaden are fished commercially for bait and for "reduction," meaning huge masses of the oily little fish are processed, "reduced" into other products—omega-3 supplements, fish meal, crop fertilizer, and livestock feed, among other things. Until recently, more than 80 percent of the entire allowable catch of menhaden for the Atlantic region was allotted to the reduction harvest; incredibly, a single company, Omega Protein, which has operated out of Reedville, Virginia, for decades, has a monopoly on the entire reduction harvest. While Omega Protein provides hundreds of jobs in Virginia, scientists, conservationists, and others have argued that not taking a longer-term approach to managing this forage species will endanger the health of the Bay as well as other commercially important fisheries, rockfish chief among them, in the future. They won a partial victory in late 2017, when regulators reduced the allowable commercial harvest for the next two years, but still declined to put certain markers in place that would lead to more active management of the fishery.

Rockfish is the dominant local fish on restaurant menus, but chefs are helping diners realize there are other fish in the Bay. I can get my bluefish fix when it's in season at Fishnet in College Park, Maryland, thanks to Turkish chef and owner Ferhat Yalcin. Whole roasted porgy is on the menu at places like Fish by José Andrés at National Harbor in Oxon Hill, Maryland, and Tail Up Goat in DC's Adams Morgan neighborhood. Everyday fish shops like the Mid-Atlantic Seafood chain serve up fried or grilled croaker, spot, butterfish, and other types known to locals who have been eating fish all their lives.

Whole porgy dressed, seasoned, and ready to roast or grill is available most days in the fish case at my neighborhood Whole Foods. Bluefish is often available at grocery store fish counters. Ivy City Smokehouse Market, a retail outlet operated by seafood wholesaler ProFish, offers seafood to the public, including a variety of local products, at the same wholesale prices DC's top chefs enjoy. Even in winter, fishmonger Dan Greenbaum was able to offer rockfish and black bass—as well as two invasive but tasty species, blue catfish (not to be confused with bluefish) and snakehead—in response to a request for local options.

Eastern Oysters and Other Shellfish

The Eastern or Virginia oyster, known scientifically as *Crassostrea virginica*, is truly the cornerstone species of the Chesapeake Bay. This oyster is found all along the Atlantic Seaboard, but it flourished in the Chesapeake Bay for millennia. Oysters have played a critical role in keeping the waters of the Bay healthy for all the other plants and animals that live there by filtering excess nitrogen, sediment, and pollution from the water along with the plankton and other tiny organisms the oysters eat. Researchers say that when English colonizers reached the Chesapeake Bay in the 1600s, the oyster population was so large that they could filter the entire nineteen trillion gallons of water in the Bay every week. It takes today's depleted community of oysters more than a year to accomplish the same task in our exponentially more polluted Bay.

Oysters were so abundant in the Bay during colonial times that their massive reefs could impede the passage of ships, and they were regarded as cheap food for the poor, much like lobsters were once used as prison food in New England. Oysters could be harvested from the shallow waters of tidal inlets and rivers by diving for them, but over time the most common way to harvest them in quantities for family use and local sale was by using oyster tongs, which look sort of like two huge rakes scissored together, with long wooden handles that reach down to the oyster beds below a boat. Above the rake teeth are metal bars, creating a basket that collects the oysters raked off the bed, letting the water drain out as the tongs are lifted out of the water. It's hard work but a pretty low-tech way to harvest a food that had been a staple for Native Americans and later for the European settlers living around the Bay.

As cities such as Annapolis, Baltimore, and Philadelphia became more populous and prosperous in the late eighteenth and early nineteenth centuries, oysters shipped in on ice became a sought-after luxury food. But the game-changer was the advent of commercial canning. The lure of profit drew oyster dredging boats to the Chesapeake Bay from New England, where the oyster beds were already suffering the effects of industrial harvesting. Oysters became the first lucrative cash crop of the Bay, creating a hard-shelled gold rush that spurred armed skirmishes dubbed "The Oyster Wars." Ultimately, the oysters themselves became the primary casualties of the war.

In order to grow, tiny juvenile oysters called "spat" must find a hard surface, to which they attach themselves permanently, within their first several weeks of life. This can be a rock or debris in the water, but the favorite and, for a time, most plentiful option was another oyster shell. Once cemented to its home base, the oyster just sits there, pumping water through its shells, filtering out both food and pollutants, releasing eggs or sperm (most oysters are both male and female at different points in their lives, so they get to do both!) into the water during the spawning season to create new spat, and generally not bothering anyone. Oysters reach maturity in two to five years and can live for many more years after that. Each baby boom of new spat attaching to old oyster shells, combined with the perfect environment created by the Bay's mixing of salt and fresh, warm and cold water, resulted, over millennia, in the giant oyster reefs that attracted other important marine life, sustained Native Americans, and astonished early European settlers.

More than twenty million bushels of oysters—that's at least two *billion* oysters—were harvested from the Bay every year during the mid-1880s, almost 40 percent of all the oysters harvested in the United States. However, as with any other exploitable natural resource that was five thousand years in the making, that level of extraction would prove to be unsustainable. Not only were the harvest numbers astronomically high, but the industrial harvest method—dredging that scraped tens of thousands of oysters off the bottom of the Bay in one go—completely destroyed entire oyster reefs that had been built up over millennia. The destruction left no foundation to which new oysters could attach and grow, not to mention very few oysters that could reproduce, disrupting the entire ecosystem dependent on those reefs, and churning tons of sediment, with no oysters to filter it, back into the Bay's waters. By the 1920s, harvests had fallen to three million bushels, and by 2002–2004, additional pressure from pollution and two diseases (MSX and Dermo, harmless to humans but devastating to oysters) had pushed the oyster harvest in the Chesapeake Bay to its lowest point ever, between one hundred thousand and two hundred thousand bushels per year.

An elegant display of oyster appetizers at the Oyster Recovery Partnership's annual Mermaid's Kiss Oyster Fest. Photo by Lauren Ewig and Jesse Snader.

However, in 2015, Bay oyster harvests reached one million bushels again for the first time in thirty years, heralding a slow comeback that owes a lot to active management of the fishery and promotion of aquaculture.

The states of Maryland and Virginia, working individually and in concert, have enacted regulations regarding the areas that can be tonged or dredged for oysters, areas that can be leased for aquaculture, and sanctuaries that are protected indefinitely and often the site of reef restoration and reseeding projects. Programs like the Oyster Recovery Partnership's Shell Recycling Alliance allow restaurants and oyster lovers to contribute to the recovery of the oyster by diverting oyster shells from the landfill or incinerator and sending them back to the Bay to be used to raise new spat. According to their website, the 30 thousand bushels of oyster shells returned through the program in 2016 will enable the planting of 150 million new oysters that will help build up reefs in the Chesapeake Bay.

Most of the oysters harvested for consumption from the Bay today are farmed. They are *Crassostrea virginica* raised in the same waters as wild oysters. The difference is that wild oysters are diploids and farmed oysters are triploids, meaning they have an extra chromosome that allows them to grow fast enough that they reach harvest size in about eighteen months. Additionally, triploid oysters are sterile, so all their energy goes into growth, not reproduction. Oysters are especially vulnerable to the devastating MSX and Dermo bacteria immediately after spawning, a hazard these oysters don't have to face. Wild oysters spawn in the months that have "r" in their names, leaving them watery and less tasty, which is the true reason why these months were said to be bad for oysters. With triploids, any month is a good month for oysters.

Triploid oyster seed is produced by breeders in hatcheries, where the spat

GMO Oysters?

Does manipulating their chromosomes make these oysters genetically modified organisms? According to a paper published by Standish Allen, who developed the triploid oyster at the Virginia Institute of Marine Science of the College of William & Mary, no DNA from other species have been introduced, nor has the DNA of the oyster itself been modified, so the answer is no:

> Although the oyster that the aquaculture industry uses is decidedly not wild, all of the changes it has undergone during domestication for aqua farming are time honored and traditional agricultural methods. One of those methods is standard selective breeding, using the genes naturally available in the wild oyster and enriching them by choosing the best offspring as broodstock for the next generation. Oysters have also been subjected to another traditional breeding trick called chromosome set manipulation, or polyploidy . . . This technique essentially supercharges the number of chromosomes contained in each cell, thereby—in most cases—supercharging the performance of the oyster on the farm. The beautiful thing about creating these "spawnless" oysters is that it is done by the simple process of crossing one oyster with another in the hatchery. There are no processes, no chemicals, no additives, no genes that don't belong, no drugs, no hormones. In short, the extra chromosomes belong to the oyster, they simply do not occur naturally in such numbers. The benefit comes from the fact that oysters spend a great deal of their energy reproducing and become weak and vulnerable during and following spawning. Take away the burden of reproduction, and they thrive on the farm.

are transplanted to oyster shells and then sold to oyster farmers, who generally raise them in floating cages. Oysters in floating cages can be protected from predators such as crabs and cownose rays, and they filter just as much water as wild oysters.

Virginia now leads the East Coast in oyster production, producing $16 million in aquaculture oysters in 2015. Maryland, which for decades surpassed Virginia in harvests of wild oysters, is working to build up its aquaculture program as well. Aquaculture allows the oysters to be protected until harvest, but it also makes them easier to bring to market, because the oysters are raised singly in the cages, rather than being allowed to remain cemented to each other in the reef system that must be chipped apart to create edible portions. Commercial oyster farms like the wildly successful Rappahannock Oyster Company, a fourth-generation oystering business made modern by cousins Ryan and Travis Croxton, also tout the "merroir" of their oysters, the unique flavors the oysters take on according to the salinity and other properties of the water they inhabit, similar to "terroir" in wines. Virginia, which has been extremely proactive in promoting its wine trails, is now promoting the Virginia Oyster Trail, highlighting eight distinct regions of Virginia oysters and the places where you can enjoy the fruits of the oyster farmers' labors, including restaurants, festivals, tours, even art using Virginia oyster shells.

Both Virginia and Maryland promote oyster gardening, where folks living along waterways raise oysters in floating cages under their docks. Various programs that help dock owners establish their oyster gardens have different goals. In some cases, you are "fostering" oyster spat, growing them until they are large enough to give back to the program for reef restoration. In others, the oysters are meant to be maintained simply to improve water quality with their filtration. In some, you can grow oysters for personal consumption. Maryland residents can even qualify for a tax credit for floating oysters on their waterfronts.

Clam aquaculture is also big business, especially in the Virginia part of the Bay. I'm not sure why it's not better known, but Virginia is first in the nation for hard-shell clam production, producing about 80 percent of the country's clams on aquaculture farms on salty inlets along Virginia's Eastern Shore. Most of these clams go to wholesalers, but chances are that almost any clams you buy at the grocery store or restaurant, unless marked otherwise, are actually pretty local.

Scallops are another mollusk that was once plentiful in the Bay, but they are hardly heard of today. They were wiped out by a catastrophic storm in 1933 and not seen again in the Bay until the Rappahannock Oyster Company took up the cause a couple of years ago. Bay scallops have proven to be more temperamental to farm than oysters, but let's hope they succeed!

The Unique Chesapeake Bay Blue Crab

Growing up in Maryland, it wasn't summer until we had crabs. Memorial Day, the Fourth of July, and Labor Day were always a good bet for a crab feast, but any old time my mother got a taste for crabs would do. We never worried about dwindling crab populations when I was young. When you see thousands upon thousands of glistening blue crabs skittering around at the wharf, clamping themselves together like in the old Barrel o' Monkeys game, trying to claw their way out of the bulging bushel baskets, it doesn't seem like they will ever end. But sometimes my parents would complain about the high price of crabs. That could have been an indication of high demand at the summer holidays, or it could have been a sign of declining catches that we weren't aware of.

When my dad finished steaming the crabs with beer and Old Bay spices, he heaped them onto newspaper-covered tables. We kids would hover at our mothers' elbows like baby birds, waiting for choice nuggets of crabmeat to be shoveled into our mouths. If you've ever picked crabs, you realize what a sacrifice this was for our crab-loving mothers. There is a whole new process of learning to love crabs, as well as an eye-opening appreciation of your mother's love, when you reach your teens and are required to pick your own crabs if you want to eat any.

Despite ongoing rumors of its imminent demise at regular intervals as I have grown up, the Chesapeake Bay blue crab is not doing so badly these days, although it continues to have its ups and downs. The blue crab winter dredge survey, conducted jointly by Maryland and Virginia each winter since 1989, is a key indicator of the health of the blue crab population. By dredging up and gathering data from hibernating crabs at specific points in the Bay, the scientists can extrapolate to a variety of numbers, including the amount of juvenile crabs, adult crabs, and female crabs of spawning age that are inhabiting the Bay. These numbers are pegged to minimum and target levels of crabs in each category believed to be required to sustain a healthy fishery.

In the first year when data was available, the winter dredge survey estimated that 791 million crabs were living in the Chesapeake Bay. That number

My dad, Vincent Brooks Jr., presides over a Brooks family backyard crab feast.
Photo by Renee Brooks Catacalos.

dropped sharply over the next ten years to a dangerously low 254 million in 2001, then rebounded slightly before hitting rock-bottom at 251 million in 2007. Writing in *Edible Chesapeake* in 2008, Kristi Bahrenburg Janzen reported on the historic emergency measures put in place Bay-wide, heavily restricting commercial and recreational harvests and curtailing the season for female crabs. "The measures are aimed at giving adult blue crabs a fighting chance to spawn. Fisheries experts say, in order for the population to rise, no more than 46 percent of the crab population should be taken each year. Between 1998 and 2002, however, the average removal rate was 68 percent, while since 2003, the rate has fallen to 55 percent on average," she wrote.

The target extraction rate for spawning-age females hovered around 40 percent during those same years, but since the establishment of a target rate of 25.5 percent in 2011, it has consistently been below that mark. The 2017 winter dredge survey estimated 455 million crabs to be living in the Bay, right at the survey's average and the second-highest total in the last 5 years.

The overfishing of blue crabs in the last decades of the twentieth century

A soft-shell crab at a peeler's shack on Taylor's Island, Maryland, under inspection by my son Louis and friend Jason Adams. Photo by Renee Brooks Catacalos.

was partially driven by the collapse of the oyster population in the 1980s. The blue crab became the most lucrative fishery in the Bay. National Marine Fisheries Service statistics show that commercial blue crab landings in Maryland and Virginia were valued at more than $43 million in 1990 and $51 million in 2002, then hit a high of $108 million in 2010 and totaled $85 million in 2015. Somewhere between 30 and 50 percent of the nation's entire production of blue crabs comes from the Chesapeake Bay.

The blue crab, *Callinectes sapidus,* translated as "beautiful savory swimmer," is found all along the Atlantic coast and around into the Gulf of Mexico, but our local blue crabs have unique culinary qualities that distinguish them from the rest of their kin. The Chesapeake Bay contains the coldest waters in the blue crab's range, causing them to put on fat stores that make the meat of the Chesapeake Bay blue crab richer and sweeter than those from warmer waters.

Soft-shell crabs are a seasonal delicacy prized by native or long-time Chesapeake eaters. Crabs grow by molting their shells periodically during their lives, allowing their bodies to expand. The soft-shell crab season runs from early May for a few months into the summer, the growth season for crabs, which essentially hibernate during the cold winter months. Once the old shell is cast off, a new shell will begin to harden within two hours. This is the window that soft-shell crab processors have to work within.

These "peeler" crabs are kept in tanks where the progress of the molting can be carefully monitored and as soon as the shell is gone, the crabs are removed from the water and refrigerated for immediate sale or frozen for shipping and year-round sale, preserving the crab in the state where it can be eaten almost whole, with just a few inedible parts removed. The entire crab can be deep-fried or sautéed. Delicious, and very clearly a blue crab.

On the other hand, crabmeat, once picked from the shell, is very hard for most eaters to distinguish as having come from a Chesapeake Bay blue crab. The crab cake also makes it too easy to eat a lot of crab without considering the effect you're having on this finite resource. If the average crab yields about two ounces of meat (yes, that's all), then a single crab cake is the equivalent of two to four crabs. If everyone had to pick those four crabs instead of having them served up in a neat little cake, we would eat far fewer of them, I'm sure.

When you know how little meat comes out of each crab, you become keenly aware that it's just not possible for the amount of crabmeat getting caked on restaurant menus to actually come from the crabs caught in the Bay. In a 2012 article in *Washington City Paper*, Jessica Sidman reported that forty-three million pounds of crabmeat are imported into Maryland each year, while the Maryland seafood industry produces less than seven hundred thousand pounds per year. The bulk of the imported crabmeat that makes its way into crab cakes comes from the blue swimming crab, *Portunus pelagicus* or others of that genus, a distant relative of the blue crab, native to the waters of Southeast Asia around Indonesia, Thailand, Vietnam, the Philippines, and China.

In the 1980s, the Phillips Seafood company, an iconic name in seafood in Maryland since 1914, began importing blue swimming crabs because they saw the decline of the Chesapeake Bay blue crab harvest. Over the years, the Asian crab population also began to be overfished, and Phillips has spearheaded a fisheries management program to keep from depleting that stock to the point of collapse as well.

Maryland has a program called True Blue, where restaurants and retailers pledge that they are using at least 75 percent Maryland blue crab meat in their establishment. It is a voluntary reporting program, but at least it gives some indication of who is willing to put their reputation on the line to back their commitment to sourcing local crabmeat. Be wary of any dish described as "Maryland style" and, even if a menu specifies Maryland crabmeat, ask whether the establishment uses *all* local crab or a mixture of local and imported. Unfortunately, restaurants sourcing their crabmeat from seafood companies in Maryland, whose reputations were built on Maryland blue crab, may not realize that most of those companies now process and package more imported crab than local product. When buying crabmeat for your own use at home, the plastic tubs of fresh crabmeat on ice at the supermarket fish counter should be labeled with the name and location of the crab house where the product was picked and processed.

As Baltimore chef, author, and ambassador of Chesapeake regional cooking John Shields describes in his many books on Chesapeake Bay cooking, there are many other delicious ways to enjoy crab in smaller quantities and on a budget. Crab soups, chowders, and bisques and

Local Seafood Directories

These resources can help you learn more about local seafood and where to buy it.

Maryland Seafood
http://seafood.maryland.gov/
Learn about the fish and shellfish available from Maryland waters, history of the seafood industry in the state, recipes for using local seafood, and features on Maryland watermen.

Old Line Fish Company
http://oldlinefish.com/
See profiles of the local watermen and -women who supply seafood for this community-supported fishery, and learn more about the species that populate the waters of the Bay.

Virginia Seafood
http://www.virginiaseafood.org/
Learn about the fish and shellfish available from Virginia waters, history of the seafood industry in the state, recipes for using local seafood, and public festivals celebrating seafood.

dishes that incorporate stuffings or fillings that feature crabmeat along with other ingredients, are great ways to stretch the crab. Using the less expensive backfin or claw meat, rather than jumbo lump crabmeat in recipes, still yields great flavor. In one of his essays, Shields advised readers to go easy on our favorite crustacean. "I'm still loving the crabs but eating less per season. The funny thing is, these infrequent feasts are more of a special occasion and

Freshly prepared soft-shell crabs at Lorraine's on Tangier Island, Virginia.
Photo by Renee Brooks Catacalos.

taste even better than ever. Likewise, to stretch our local crabs and our crab dollars, I would suggest keeping the crab cake—which we Chesapeake folks expect to be practically all crab with no filler—for special dinners."

Whether you prefer hard-shell, soft-shell, or crabmeat already picked, prices reflect the hard work that goes into crab harvesting and processing. Crabs can't be scooped up from the bottom of the Bay by industrial machines, and they can't be farmed, due to the way they migrate and the fact that they eat each other when kept too long in close quarters. The men and women who work the water must go out in their boats and put out pots and lines in the water daily to catch crabs. For crabmeat, no machine can match the work of experienced crab pickers. Ironically, some observers think the dwindling pool of human labor is a bigger threat to the Chesapeake Bay crabbing industry than the difficulties of the crabs themselves. I saw signs of this myself when I visited Smith Island, Maryland, and Tangier Island, Virginia, isolated communities in the middle of the Chesapeake Bay whose existence has been defined and sustained by working the water, men crabbing and oystering, women picking crabmeat. The population of these islands is dwindling, as is the land mass of the islands themselves. Both communities are exploring ways to diversify to maintain their footholds in the Bay, from the Smith Island cakes that have been named the official Maryland state dessert to the forays into oyster aquaculture taking place on Tangier Island.

On the Eastern Shore, the Chesapeake Bay's legendary fishing and processing towns, such as Cambridge and Crisfield in Maryland and Reedville in the Northern Neck and towns near the mouth of the Bay in Virginia, are no longer the bustling places they once were either, and the faces of the industry are changing. Historical museums and books chronicle how black men once made up much of the labor force that worked on Chesapeake Bay boats and docks. Women, black and white, picked crabmeat and shucked oysters at the big processing companies. Now, unable to fill these jobs anymore from the local communities, crab processors depend on women from a few towns in Mexico who return to the Eastern Shore each year under the guest worker visa program to keep them going through the crab-picking season.

Given all the indignities we've inflicted on it over the last several centuries, the Chesapeake Bay has proven to be remarkably resilient. So has the dream of working the water. The people supplying clams, oysters, crabs, and rockfish to Old Line Fish Company, the mid-Atlantic's first subscription-based community-supported fishery, have decades of experience in communities on the water and include a husband-and-wife team that also gives heritage boat tours to show visitors a closer look at the life of the Bay's "watermen." The cousins behind the Rappahannock Oyster Company grew up in an oystering family but took detours that allowed them to bring new entrepreneurial spirit to their revival of the family business. Ronald Williams is a young black entrepreneur who did not grow up in a farming or fishing family but felt drawn to both pursuits, leading him to raise cattle and start a crabbing operation, selling these and other local foods directly to customers in Prince George's County, Maryland.

These are the kinds of producers who make me hopeful about the future of the Chesapeake seafood industry and excited about trying more of the foods of our local waters.

Roasted Whole Porgy or Black Bass

Both porgy and black bass are mild, meaty white fish, perfect for lots of different recipes. But nothing could be easier than roasting these fish whole, with the heads and tails. Fish are quite similar to chicken in the way that cooking the entire animal, with the bones, skin, and, in the case of fish, heads and tails, imparts so much more flavor and nutritional value than you get from a boneless, skinless chicken breast or fish fillet. Porgies and black bass are smallish fish, from 1 to 3 pounds. You lose a lot of good meat along the tail and under the cheeks and head when you fillet them.

Just have your fish seller gut and scale the fish, and you'll be ready to go.

2 whole fish, 1 to 1½ pounds each
Olive oil
Salt and pepper
Small bunch mixed fresh herbs—such as thyme, rosemary, and oregano
1 lemon, quartered

Preheat the oven to 400°F.

Make two or three scores with a sharp knife on each side of the fish. Rub the fish with a few teaspoons of olive oil and season inside and out with salt and pepper. Spread one-third of the herbs in a baking dish and place the fish on top of the herbs. Stuff some of the herbs in the cavity of each fish, and lay the rest of the herbs on top of the fish. Lightly squeeze a lemon wedge over each fish, then tuck the squeezed wedge into the cavity with the herbs.

Roast the fish for 20-25 minutes, until the skin gets slightly crispy and the flesh is firm, but not dry. Serves 2.

5 | To Market

In the summer of 2006, I was driving 40 miles round-trip each week to pick up my community-supported agriculture (CSA) share at Clagett Farm in Upper Marlboro, Maryland. The share was plentiful in greens, squashes, cucumbers, melons, tomatoes, and root vegetables, but it didn't include tree fruit like peaches or apples, and it was light on berries unless you picked extra yourself. So I also visited up to four farmers markets each week to buy fruit, bread, cider, cheese, and vegetables the CSA didn't grow a lot of, such as corn. My usual rotation included Riverdale Park on Thursdays, Silver Spring on Saturdays, and Takoma Park and/or Greenbelt on Sundays, with occasional stops at Hyattsville on Tuesdays or any market taking place in a town I was visiting or traveling through. There were no meat vendors at the markets then, so I would drive more than 100 miles round-trip to buy 40-pound boxes of meat at Springfield Farm in Baltimore County every month. I supplemented these forays with local milk, honey, and eggs that I could buy at the Takoma Park Silver Spring Co-Op or MOM's Organic Market during the week. And this was all *before* I started publishing *Edible Chesapeake* and could justify my extreme shopping habits as a work-related requirement.

Today in 2018, enjoying local food has mellowed from being an adventure sport requiring special training, knowledge, and equipment to a recreational pursuit that can be practiced as time and money allow, with satisfying results. The success of farmers markets as the gateway to eating local has spurred greater demand from demographically and socioeconomically diverse consumers. This has sparked new responses from producers, as well as diversification in the ways they get their product to markets. Farmers markets still provide a tangible and emotional anchor for the local food movement, but the farmers market model is evolving, making way for the expansion of other ways of selling directly to consumers, as well as a more robust retail, restaurant, and wholesale pipeline for local food.

Farmers Markets

According to the US Department of Agriculture, 67 percent of direct farm sales to consumers take place through on-farm stores and farmers markets. Although that information is not broken down specifically for our area, farmers markets in the major population centers reach more people than do rural farm stands in our region.

The presence of the farmers who produced the food they are selling is what makes a farmers market unique. But the primary job of farmers is to grow food and, generally, they need to be on their farms to do that, which is why the days and hours of farmers markets can seem limited. To be sure, they have to spend time harvesting, processing, and packing the food, whether they put it on a truck to a wholesaler or on a truck for the farmers market. But going to a farmers market also carries the risk that they might not be able to sell everything they load up, and it requires a full day off the farm for at least one staffer, if not two or more. The cost-benefit analysis of going to a farmers market only works for the farmer if there is a critical mass of regular customers who can be counted on to shop every week and to pay a fair price for what the farmer has grown.

All consumers are not alike, and neither are all farmers markets. They can run the gamut from three or four farmers or market gardeners setting up their produce on card tables in a church parking lot to dozens of stalls of veggies, fruits, dairy, meat, and all manner of prepared foods and musical entertainment. My friend Rana Koll-Mandell refers to her Garrett Park "farmer market" because there is only one farm, but that's all the neighborhood needs. What's important is that the market's foundation is fresh food, grown or produced within a reasonably local distance, whether that's the hyper-local urban hoop-house farm a few blocks away or a rural farm 50 or 100 miles outside the city.

As we've discussed, proximity is not the only factor in defining what's local. We want food that was grown to be consumed by local people, with respect for our local ecosystems, and that contributes to our local economy and community well-being. This is why "producer-only" markets require that the people selling the food be owners or employees of the farms that produced the food *and* that they sell only what they produced on their own farms, so

Bev Eggleston (in sunglasses) dishes up "the South in your mouth" at the Dupont Circle FRESHFARM Market. Photo by Renee Brooks Catacalos.

they can speak knowledgeably to consumers about their food and their production methods. Items that do not grow locally, such as bananas or oranges, cannot be offered at a producer-only market. Offering something unusual for the region or out of character for the farm, such as a meat farmer suddenly having cantaloupes for sale, might prompt a farm verification visit from market staff or volunteers.

However, even the most rigorously enforced markets have introduced some flexibility over the years. FRESHFARM Markets was a stickler for its producer-only rules in its first few years but made changes over time to allow for artisanal products, such as cheese made from local milk and fermented products made from local produce, rather than requiring that the maker also be the farmer, which was not practical as small farmstead food businesses ramped up to meet demand.

Markets that offer ready-to-eat foods may encourage or require those vendors to use locally grown produce and locally raised meats, especially those for sale by the market's own farm vendors. Coffee seems to be essential to the enjoyment of the farmers market experience and helps keep shoppers at

Public Markets

Eastern Market and the Maine Avenue Fish Market in Washington, DC; Lexington Market, Avenue Market, and others in Baltimore; Reading Terminal Market in Philadelphia—these are historic public food markets. Traditionally, they were hubs of commerce for local farmers as well as butchers, fishmongers, and purveyors of specialty foods from near and far. Public food markets were critically important in the nineteenth and early twentieth centuries, providing one-stop convenience for shoppers, but also a central location where cities could regulate the quality of edible goods being sold to the public.

Baltimore still operates six of what were once eleven public markets and has the oldest continuously operating public market system in the country. Anchored by the "world-famous" Lexington Market, which dates to 1782, these markets are searching for new identities that fit better with their changing neighborhoods and with the changing local food system. There are homestyle bakeries where you can still get a cupcake for one dollar alongside meat stalls selling scrapple, hog maws, chitterlings, pigs feet, rabbit, and piles and piles of chicken parts. Faidley Seafood has been in Lexington Market since 1886 and is still famous for its crab cakes and local seafood. But many of the occupied stalls (and there are many that are vacant) are carry-outs offering fried foods, deli sandwiches, and Chinese food. Most of the markets have only one or two fresh produce stands.

"We want to transition the markets into having more staple foods and less prepared food," said Holly Freishtat, food policy director for Baltimore. Public markets are a key part of the strategy to address the lack of fresh, healthy food in lower-income neighborhoods, a role markets historically played in cities. The Avenue Market in West Baltimore "is a top priority among our public markets," Freishtat said, pointing to the work being done by the community-driven No Boundaries Coalition to launch a locally sourced produce stand at Avenue Market, as well as other initiatives to support farmers and food entrepreneurs from the surrounding neighborhoods.

DC's Maine Avenue Fish Market on the southwest waterfront is the oldest continuously operating public fish market in the country. Natives of the region have always called it "The Wharf," but that name has now been claimed by the new development that has been built around the fish stalls, so I guess we now have to call it the Fish Market. Dayboats used to pull right up to these docks to sell their catch. Today, the market is a small complex of permanently anchored floating barges where you can buy fresh seafood to take home or have it cooked for you on the spot. The main vendors, Captain White's and Jessie Taylor, are family businesses that have been at the Wharf—sorry, the Fish Market—for decades. Freshly shucked oysters, bushels of blue crabs, dozens of kinds of fish from the Chesapeake and beyond are for sale every day, along with steamed crabs and shrimp, fried whiting sandwiches, and other ready-to-eat seafood meals.

Eastern Market on Capitol Hill is the only public fresh food market remaining in Washington, DC. Who knew there was once a Center Market and a Western Market? Or that the O Street Market—now-redeveloped as City Market at O— was once known as Northern Market, and the building now occupied by Dean and Deluca was Georgetown Market? Eastern Market hosts an open-air farmers market on Tuesdays and weekends, in addition to the permanent stalls selling meats, cheeses, baked goods, produce, and specialty foods inside. Most of the farmers who participate in the farmers market grow their own produce, but some also aggregate produce grown by other farms in the region.

the market longer, so markets make an exception for the raw ingredients as long as the coffee beans are roasted locally. Likewise with bread and pastries, where local grains are not common but accent ingredients like fruits, honey, butter, and milk can and should come from local sources. Some markets also make exceptions for locally owned businesses that produce olives and olive oil from family-owned groves outside the region or for locally based fishers who sell wild-caught Alaskan seafood. Look on a market's website or ask the market manager about their producer requirements if you want to know more.

Urban farmers or beginning farmers without access to large amounts of land may not always be able to produce large-enough quantities of produce or a wide-enough variety to participate in farmers markets on their own. To encourage and support these businesses, which represent the future of the local food system, some markets allow two or more farms to sell their products cooperatively. This lets them have a fuller display to better serve customers and lets them share market-day responsibilities while tending to their farming operations. It is also a way for smaller communities to get farmers markets started when demand may be lower.

There are a few markets in Virginia, such as the Virginia Beach Farmers Market, that are open daily all year, with local farmers and other vendors who have permanent stalls, as well as daily truck farmers during the season. Richmond's 17th Street Market was traditionally open with farm vendors Thursday through Sunday. A major renovation that has disrupted the market for several years is slated to add more restaurants and a pedestrian plaza to an updated market pavilion site in 2018. The closest to a permanent farmers market I've found in Maryland is the Bethesda Farm Women's Co-Op, which has a mix of indoor and outdoor vendors, including a few farms, plus artisan purveyors like Stonyman Gourmet Farmer's cheese stall, among other types of food and craft products. The market is open several days a week, but individual vendor hours vary.

Sometimes when I mention farmers markets to people, they respond by telling me how much they love going to the Amish market, without realizing that we are not talking about the same thing. Amish markets often feature cheeses, produce, and some meats from Amish farms, but they also offer a lot of prepared foods, homemade baked goods, candies, and bulk ingredients that are not local and not produced by the vendors. They are not, strictly speaking, farmers markets. If eating locally grown food is your goal, you'll want to ask the vendors about their sources—maybe the homemade fudge is made with local cream. Also, although there are many organic or sustainable Amish and Mennonite farms in the area, don't assume the food is produced sustainably based on the prohibition against the use of electricity and modern clothing fasteners. There is no religious prohibition on the use of chemicals or genetically modified organisms, so if growing methods are important to you and you are shopping at an Amish market, ask the same questions you would of any other farmer.

Farmers markets have become more common in low-income communities, both urban and rural, as the ability of farmers and markets to accept various forms of federal nutrition benefits as payment has become more widespread, thanks to continued activism on the part of food justice and health advocates, along with market managers and farmers who see the need to make healthy food available to those who have least access to it. Crossroads Farmers Market in the heavily Latino neighborhood of Langley Park, Maryland, is a nationwide model for creating a market that reflects and responds to its community, recruiting and training growers and food producers from within the community alongside more seasoned farmers market growers to provide a mix of offerings that are affordable and culturally appropriate for their customers.

Food benefits are just like money to the farmers' bottom lines, and most are happy to accept them, although there is work to be done to reduce the extra time and effort—and sometimes equipment or staff expense—required to process these benefits, through better alignment of federal, state, and local procedures. Advocates do a great deal of community outreach and education to increase farmers market redemption of federal food benefits as well as state and privately funded programs that match federal benefit dollars spent.

Roadside Stands and On-Farm Stores

Roadside farm stands dot the rural landscapes of our childhood memories, even if they may be fewer and farther between on drives through the Eastern Shore or central Virginia today. Those that remain continue to be great ways to buy from local farms. They can range from just a couple of benches of tomatoes or corn on the side of the road to barn-sized buildings with refrigerated and frozen products, as well as fresh produce. And some are closer to our daily city commutes than we might think.

Fields of strawberries, tomatoes, and other crops surround Spicknall's Farm Market, not far outside the Capital Beltway in Beltsville, Maryland. During the season, they sell their own produce as well as crops and items like popcorn sourced from other farms in the area. A dozen or more varieties of apples grow in the 5-acre orchard surrounding the store at Heyser Farms, in

At Heyser Farms' farm store in Montgomery County, Maryland, suburban consumers can buy fresh apples and other fruit, as well as unpasteurized apple cider and apple cider donuts in the fall. Photo by Kristi Bahrenburg Janzen.

99 | To Market

One of the many colors of watermelon at the Councell Farms roadside farm market on Maryland's Eastern Shore.
Photo by Renee Brooks Catacalos.

Silver Spring, Maryland, just a half-mile north of the Inter-County Connector highway. This is one of the few places where you can still buy unpasteurized apple cider, pressed onsite in the fall, when they also make apple cider donuts. The store is open through the winter, selling local dairy and meats, homemade pies, jams, and fruit butters, and local apples and pears.

Norman's Farm Market, which operates roadside stands along busy commuting roads in Bethesda, Chevy Chase, and Rockville, began as a reseller of small-farm produce. In recent years, they have acquired their own farms and started growing their own produce as well. Working with several small, family-owned farms in Maryland, Pennsylvania, and Virginia ensures a large-enough supply of local products throughout the season that they can operate three daily farm stands and a CSA.

Willowsford Farm is a working farm that was built as an amenity in the center of the Willowsford master-planned community in Loudoun County, Virginia. The Willowsford Farm Stand is open five days a week during the season, offering produce, eggs, and honey from the farm, a pick-your-own garden of culinary and medicinal herbs, dairy and meat from nearby farms, and even ready-for-the-oven prepared foods made by the community's culinary staff using farm-stand ingredients.

It's not unusual to see a crab truck or stand along the highway on the Eastern Shore or Southern Maryland in the summer, but many more are hidden down the side roads and creeks in waterside communities along the Bay. On a summer visit to Cambridge, Maryland, our friends Geoff and Shanta took my family down winding roads to their favorite crab shack on Taylor's Island. We checked out the "peeler" tanks where the soft-shell crabs go through their stages of molting, and we bought both hard- and soft-shell live crabs to cook. Very few of these seafood shacks have websites or listings in local food directories. Once you find one, be sure to take the phone number, get on their email list, or find their Facebook page if you want to stay in the loop.

Community-Supported Agriculture

If going to the farmers market could be called a flirtation with local food, buying a CSA share is like going steady. No matter what, you have a date with a box of local vegetables every single week for months, without a break, no matter what is in the box, because you have paid for the privilege, sight unseen, before the season even began.

CSAs in the 1980s used to include required volunteer hours working on the farm as well as the up-front payment that helps small farmers cover the costs of getting their crops in before they would normally have any cash flow. These days, CSAs may offer the opportunity to work on the farm as a volunteer or as a way to pay for all or part of a share, but few require it. The rest of the model, however, is the same, with CSA participants receiving an equitable portion of the farm's produce for the season, which means sharing equally in the burden of harvest failures. If deer driven onto the farm by nearby construction activity take a bite out of every sweet potato in the field, everyone loses their sweet potatoes for that year, with no refund. This actually happened during one year of my CSA at Clagett Farm in Upper Marlboro, Maryland. But in another year, there was a bumper crop of tomatoes, too many for the farm staff and volunteers to pick for our regular shares, so they gave us the option to pick as many more tomatoes as we pleased. In about

Gail Taylor displays a small CSA share from her DC urban farm, Three Part Harmony Farm. Photo by Michelle Scholtes.

20 minutes, I picked more than 40 pounds of beautiful, ripe red tomatoes, some of which I canned as sauce and some of which I froze whole to throw into soups and chili during the winter, all at no extra cost.

CSAs grew at least as fast as farmers markets until also experiencing a plateau in 2016. Perhaps the market was tapped out of customers willing and able to part with hundreds of dollars in early spring, right after the holidays and before tax return season, for vegetables they wouldn't see for another two to three months. A bigger challenge could be customers not always possessing both the kitchen skills and the appetite to store, cook, and eat the volume of vegetables they receive each week. Lots of people are surprised by how the veggies can overwhelm them, if they haven't planned ahead.

A head of leafy lettuce or a bag of spring mix, two or three bunches of spring onions, a pint of strawberries, and some radishes in a typical early spring share might have the new CSA shareholder wondering whether it's going to be worth it. The first few summer shares containing a couple of bunches of kale or collards, five or six bell peppers, two or three large zucchini or zephyr squash, paper bags full of small hot peppers, a pound or two of tomatoes, a bulb of kohlrabi, and one or two other items seem manageable and satisfying. After a couple of weekends at the beach, though, people start to fall behind and increasingly find themselves taking "the walk of shame" to the compost pile with veggies that wilted from neglect.

As fall progresses, the shares get ever heavier with watermelons, sweet potatoes, butternut and other winter squash, late-harvest tomatoes, potatoes, maybe storage onions, and garlic. These crops last longer but are more masses of food to cook just as people are looking for quick weekday meals as school and sports schedules kick back in and work gears up from any summer lull.

Farmers sometimes find it hard to believe that people aren't able to use all the vegetables in their shares. DC farmer Gail Taylor told me the shares her customers receive from her Three Part Harmony Farm CSA "would be one meal for me!" But CSA farmers have responded to customer needs, recognizing that the value to the shareholder is not in the volume of vegetables alone, and for some customers, less is more. CSAs now offer whole, half, and splittable shares to accommodate singles, couples, families, and others who want to pool costs. More CSAs also offer convenient pick-up points off the farm, at farmers markets, office buildings, or neighborhood locations, and many deliver directly to customers' homes.

Produce farms can no longer claim a monopoly on CSAs. Meat producers are discovering that the CSA model can work very well for them. Since meat can be frozen, farmers can set their own slaughter schedules and keep the meat on hand for distribution in CSA shares as needed. It allows for customers to make a limited number of choices about what goes in their share each month, based on availability, but there is no risk to the farmer or the customer of having the food in their share go bad before they can use it.

Lori Hill at Cabin Creek Heritage Farm in Upper Marlboro, Maryland, said freezer space was always a concern for people who wanted to buy her family's pastured poultry, beef, and lamb in bulk, but attending a dozen farmers markets to sell meat by the cut was excessively time-consuming. With their CSA, buyers choose the right size share for their family, from 5 to 20 pounds, made up of a single type of meat or a combination of meats. Members pay up front for a four-month season. They get a share once a month, either at the farm or a farmers market. Cabin Creek raises most of the animals on their own farm but collaborates with Evermore Farm in Carroll County, Maryland, for the grass-fed beef, an arrangement that takes advantage of Evermore's rural grazing land and Cabin Creek's proximity to DC-area consumers.

At the extreme locavore end of the CSA spectrum, Rob and Maureen Moutoux at Moutoux Orchards in Purcellville, Virginia, were the first farm-

Stores That Source Locally

I don't have any scientific criteria for determining who qualifies to be on this list. Basically, if I can find more than one local product in each of the fresh food parts of the store—produce, dairy, meat, seafood—every time I go there, they make my list. These are the ones I am most familiar with, but I'm sure there are others yet to discover.

Chesapeake's Bounty
North Beach and St. Leonard, MD

Sources 100 percent of the products in its two small Southern Maryland stores from the Chesapeake region, including all kinds of local fish, crabs and shellfish.

Shucked local oysters for sale at Chesapeake's Bounty in North Beach, Maryland. Photo courtesy of Chesapeake's Bounty.

Common Market
Frederick, MD

Great variety of meats, seafood, lots of dairy, and vegetables from local producers, including some produce grown on its own nearby farm, as well as local ginger beer on tap.

Dawson's Market
Rockville, MD

Uses labels to rate produce as "Local–Good," "Local–Better," or "Local–Best," depending on a combination of distance and growing methods; hosts a farmers market and sells local beer on tap.

Glen's Garden Market
Dupont Circle and Adams Morgan, DC

Catering to busy young urbanites, Glen's has a focus on prepared foods and entertaining, featuring a large number of local cheeses, jams, condiments, beers, and other beverages.

Maple Avenue Market
Vienna, VA

Along with local dairy and meats, stocks only seasonal produce, including greenhouse-grown produce in winter, from the owners' own farm and other Virginia producers.

MOM's Organic Market
Multiple locations in MD, DC, and VA

Most fresh meats are from local and organic sources, along with seasonal produce, eggs, dairy, tofu, jam, and honey, plus several local ice cream brands.

Takoma Park Silver Spring Co-op
Takoma Park, MD

Frozen meat from Takoma Park Farmers Market vendors, local tofu, eggs, dairy, and produce, and BeeGeorge Honey from backyard hives in and around Takoma Park.

ers in the Chesapeake to launch a whole-diet CSA (the only other I'm aware of is offered by Groundworks Farm in Pittsville on Maryland's Eastern Shore). The whole-diet CSA provides a year-round share, for an entire family, of dairy, meats, fruits, vegetables, and some grains from their own farm and a handful of neighboring producers. On their website, they say, "Simply put, you can think of it like homesteading with us, like being part of the family and having the same access to all of the abundance of foods that we enjoy out here on the farm."

I visited on a pick-up day and watched members drive up to the farm shed with armfuls of reusable shopping bags, just as I do when I go to the grocery store. Inside the cool of the open-sided shed, there were tables piled with a bountiful display of seasonal vegetables, berries, and fruits. There were bins of wheat, buckwheat, rye, millet, and barley flour. Cheese from a neighboring farm was available, as was a large insulated dispenser of raw milk from Rob's own dairy herd. Members filled their own jugs from the milk tap—the CSA includes a cow share, an arrangement that allows farmers and consumers

Nicole Donnelly grabs what she can during peach season at Takoma Park Farmers Market. Photo courtesy of Black Rock Orchard.

to get around federal laws that prohibit the commercial sale of unpasteurized milk for human consumption. I saw a sign on the freezer stocked with wrapped pieces of beef, pork, lamb, and chicken, giving loose guidelines for how much to take per family. Everything else was "free choice," open for members to take as much as they wanted.

Rob told me the members understand that they are part of a food community and pretty much self-regulate their consumption. I didn't see anyone loading up as if they were trying to maximize their value at an all-you-can-eat buffet. They were thoughtful and appreciative of the food available. One member explained that she moves in and out of the DC area for professional reasons every few years, and whenever she is here she lobbies to regain a coveted spot in this always sold-out CSA. "It's worth the drive," she said of her current weekly commute to Loudoun County from Maryland, especially because the share includes the farm's raw milk.

Buying Bulk On-Farm

You can still buy the old-fashioned way from some farms—with bulk orders that are discounted based on how much you buy. Meat farmers will still sell you a whole or half lamb or pig, a side or a quarter of beef (usually a lateral quarter, which gives you a mix of cuts from the front and back quarters). Most will also offer bulk boxes of anywhere from 15 to 50 pounds of meat, if you want something a little smaller than a quarter. Bulk meat is normally ordered in advance and may take several weeks to be ready, based on the slaughtering, aging, and butchering schedule. You can normally express preferences for certain things, such as what percentage of your order should be roasts versus ground meat, or what type of sausage you would like, or whether you want any organ meats. For meat eaters with freezer space or two or three friends to split the order with, buying meat in bulk is still the most economical way to source local.

Produce can be purchased in bulk also. I have ordered half-bushels of apples from a farmer one week and picked them up at the farmers market the next. I've picked up half-bushels of sweet potatoes from Eastern Shore farm stands in early November, just before they close for the season. Perishable produce like tomatoes, peaches, and apples are popular bulk purchases for canning, freezing, or drying. Storage produce like potatoes, sweet potatoes, onions, and garlic, can be kept for weeks or months when properly stored in a cool dry place like a root cellar, basement, or porch protected from freezing.

Farm Co-ops and Delivery Boxes

A number of food system studies have confirmed what Tom McDougall, founder of 4P Foods, said to a group exploring how to expand the local food distribution system: "The amount of food that is moving into our local food system is a fraction of what it could be." We can't open enough farmers markets or CSAs to push local food consumption in our area out of the single digits. Our area is too densely populated for everyone to be able to get a significant portion of their food directly from a farmer.

Not every local farmer wants to deal with dozens or hundreds of individual consumers every week either. Some farmers just want to grow the best food they can and leave it to someone else to sell it to the people who will appreciate it. Consumers who don't shop at farmers markets or don't cook at home might still like to support local producers, if they could do it more easily. Into this breach have stepped companies like 4P Foods, based in DC and working primarily with Virginia producers, Garrett Growers Cooperative in Garrett County, Maryland, and Lancaster Farm Fresh Cooperative from Pennsylvania. These companies gather, or aggregate, food from many local farms, to package and deliver it in ways that offer more convenience for consumers and some wholesale customers as well.

"I started 4P Foods because I realized that my friends were never going to subscribe to a CSA," says Tom McDougall. But he believed his millennial friends would eat more local food if it were more convenient and predictable to get. Delivery programs such as 4P Foods, Washington's Green Grocer, and Hometown Harvest (affiliated with South Mountain Creamery, which offers home delivery of milk from its Western Maryland dairy) are not CSAs, but they offer regularly scheduled delivery of boxes of produce, dairy, meat, and other products directly to homes and offices. They work with farmers to create varied, convenient, year-round access to local foods, either throughout all their shares or through local-only options. Deliveries can be skipped and rescheduled, and some box items can be switched out or added, all through online portals. They cater to consumers who want to eat local but want more convenience and are okay with not personally meeting every farmer.

I want to mention Hungry Harvest here as well, a locally based company that delivers very affordable boxes of perfectly edible produce rescued from the wholesale food chain. They say that they care more about keeping the food from going to waste than where it's grown, but the majority of what they source during our local growing season does come from local producers.

Lancaster Farm Fresh Cooperative is a cooperative of three hundred small farms in Lancaster County, Pennsylvania, that delivers its CSA to thousands of consumers in the Baltimore-Washington area. Members do pay up front for the season, as in a traditional CSA, but instead of all the items coming from one farm, the farmers aggregate their products to maintain consistent supplies, regardless of crop failure at any single farm. This also lets the farmers market cooperatively rather than competitively and to instead put their energy into growing their products. Lancaster Farm Fresh shareholders might not get the direct contact with a single farm that many people treasure in the CSA model, but they do get reliability and convenience.

Old Line Fish Company is the region's first community-supported fishery (CSF), operated by the Annapolis-based Oyster Recovery Partnership since 2015. The Oyster Recovery Partnership works to restore the Bay's oyster population for the benefit of the oysters, the water quality of the Bay, and the livelihood of those who work the waters and sees promoting responsible consumption of local Bay species as a way to involve consumers. The Old Line Fish CSF is paid in advance and provides a biweekly share of seafood aggregated directly from small suppliers working in Maryland waters.

During the 2017 summer season, I subscribed to the Old Line CSF and received a rotating selection of oysters, both live in the shell and shucked, rockfish and blue catfish fillets, live soft-shell crabs, and fresh crabmeat. I was hoping the CSF would encourage me to try new foods, one of the things that attracts me about vegetable CSAs. And it did, to a degree. I had never handled live oysters at home before. While I still shied away from eating them raw, I did learn how to roast them in the oven to pop their shells, then incorporate them into a delicious, creamy oyster stew. Likewise, I cleaned and cooked soft-shell crabs for the first time, with the help of my son, Louis, who has never been squeamish about showing a crab who's boss. I did, however, choose to take a substitution when long-necked soft-shell clams were in the share!

I was just a little disappointed not to receive other types of fish in the share. Kelly Barnes of the Oyster Recovery Partnership explained that buying in consumer quantities directly from watermen can be a challenge, even with the Partnership's connections. "They are not used to selling direct to consumers, so we can only get the quantities they can spare," she said. The CSF also tended toward products that required minimal processing to keep them fresh for the pick-up, which made it more difficult to work with smaller fish species like croakers or porgies that would have taken more time to gut and scale.

Restaurants that claim to source local get so much attention from the media and casual diners that "localwashing" has become rampant. I've heard many farmers complain over the years about restaurants (and stores) who purchased a few pounds of lettuce or kale from them once or twice but kept the farm name on their marketing materials long after they stopped buying product. Another common practice is to base a local-sourcing claim on the purchase of garnish items like pea shoots, microgreens, or edible flowers. These crops can be great revenue generators for urban farms and specialty growers, so it's great for a restaurant to buy them, but as the only local items on the menu, they are merely window dressing.

I've mentioned in other chapters some of the restaurants that have been locally sourcing well for some time, but I want to highlight two unique examples of restaurateurs who have made extraordinary commitments to local sourcing, at very different scales that reach completely different sets of diners.

Spike Gjerde goes further than just about anyone in his zeal for local throughout his growing constellation of food enterprises: Woodberry Kitchen, his flagship Baltimore restaurant; Parts and Labor Butchery, a full-service butcher shop and casual dining spot, also in Baltimore; and A Rake's Progress in DC, opened in early 2018. If it can't be made from local ingredients, you won't find it on his menus. Woodberry Kitchen has been called the Chez Panisse of the mid-Atlantic—a pilgrimage site for worshippers of local food. Citrus juices have been replaced by *verjus*, an acidic seasoning made from grapes that goes back to Roman times. The restaurant makes and cans its own tomato sauce, tomato paste, mustard, pickles, jams, and condiments during the summer glut for use in the winter. Woodberry Pantry jams, fish pepper sauce, and other condiments are also available for sale at stores that source locally and online at the restaurant's website. Spike and the butchering staff at his restaurants have put thousands of hours of practice and research into determining how to maximize the use of whole animals in their kitchens, in order to give farmers the prices they deserve and customers the superlative dining experiences they've come to expect. Farmers love Spike Gjerde and he shows his love for them and their products on every plate.

On the other end of the spectrum, Ype Von Hengst, executive chef and cofounder of the Silver Diner chain, with fourteen restaurants in Maryland, Virginia, and New Jersey, spent $1 million to revamp the company's menus about ten years ago, eliminating trans fats while incorporating healthier recipes and locally sourced ingredients. His purchasing leverage with regional food distributors enabled him to convince them to create special routes to bring the produce, dairy, and meats he wanted from farms and farm cooperatives in Maryland, Virginia, and Pennsylvania. The volume of meals his chain produces requires that Ype work with larger suppliers than those that work with Spike Gjerde. But Ype has said just because they have more than one restaurant, it doesn't mean they can't make a commitment to local sourcing. That commitment means thousands of diners every day are eating local without even having to think about it.

Foodservice Buyers

Catering companies, school cafeterias, and hotel and hospital kitchens generally fall into the category of institutional buyers of food, who need an assist from a middleman (see the next section) to get local ingredients and products into their kitchens. But that's not always the case.

Sourcing for catering can be tricky because people are booking events with specific menus far in advance. Josh Carin of Geppetto Catering in Riverdale Park, Maryland, started working with producers at the Riverdale Park Farmers Market more than a decade ago, purchasing meat for his barbecue operation. However, he soon realized that his capacity to process and store products for future use could be put to good use to buy excess production from several of the Maryland farms at the market. Chicken and pork from Groff's Content Farm in Frederick and salad greens from ECO City Farms in Edmonston can always be slipped onto the catering menu. He also buys up peaches and tomatoes, sometimes 40 bushels at a time, from Blades Orchard in Federalsburg. If they aren't used for his current menus, he freezes them or makes sauce and other preparations that can be stored.

When I heard that St. Mary's County farmer David Paulk of Sassafras Creek Farm had something like a ton of organic sweet potatoes from a bumper crop that he hadn't been able to move, I let Josh know, and he swooped in and bought up the whole lot, some of which went into hors d'oeuvres at an architecture awards event he catered for me later that fall. He drives a hard bargain to make it economically feasible for his business, but also keeps the farmers from taking a loss on product that might otherwise end up going to animal feed or being composted.

School districts in agricultural counties, where the ratio of local farms to local schools is high and the distances between local farms and local schools are short, are often able to do a great job at bringing local food to the school cafeteria. Locally produced orchard fruits, lettuces, and other salad items are among popular purchases, based on their availability as well as the ability to serve them without much prep. One of the challenges faced by some school districts is the lack of cooking kitchens that might give them the tools to use a wider variety of products, like potatoes and meats.

Large, urban districts share the challenge of cooking facilities, compounded by the sheer numbers of students they have to feed. The logistics of getting food from farms to these districts' central distribution points and out to hundreds of schools, at a price point they can afford, severely limits how much farm-to-school activity goes on outside of fall promotional events such as Maryland Homegrown School Lunch Week and Virginia Farm to School Week. Cities like DC and Baltimore are trying to make it easier by partnering with food hubs and adopting "Good Food Purchasing" policies that support the procurement of healthy, local produce.

Hospital food has been the butt of almost as many jokes as school food, but local food activists through groups like Health Care Without Harm's Healthy Food In Health Care initiative have been working in that arena as well. An institution such as Union Hospital of Cecil County in Maryland that is not part of a larger healthcare system is not constrained by the same layers of purchasing contracts and restrictions. Food and Nutrition Services Manager Holly Emmons has been nationally recognized many times over for her work in shifting Union Hospital's purchasing policies and cooking strategies to emphasize sustainably produced meats and produce in both patient and visitor meals, to the point where she is purchasing close to 50 percent of her food ingredients from local, sustainable sources. The hospital executed direct-purchase contracts with Maryland farms, including Liberty Delight Farms for its beef and Priapi Gardens, which was able to build additional greenhouses for expansion of its Certified Organic vegetables as a result of its commitments from Union Hospital.

Auctions, Distributors, and Food Hubs Fuel Farm-to-Institution Buying

Author and journalist Sam Fromartz provided a guest article to *Edible Chesapeake* in 2008 called "Middlemen on a Mission." In it, he described the work of three organizations in different parts of the country, including Pennsylvania's Tuscarora Organic Growers Cooperative (TOG), that had been "chip-

Food Halls

On the site of the former DC Farmers Market in DC's Florida Avenue wholesale district, Union Market is the city's premier example of one of the latest nationwide food trends, the food hall. With artisan food producers and a variety of prepared food concepts, food halls are like destination food courts, without the need for a mall because all the shopping and entertainment options you might need are provided within the food hall itself. The Rappahannock Oyster Company's raw bar is the center of market action, and the liquor store Cordial carries a number of local labels. If you want to buy actual raw ingredients, check out butchers Red Apron and Harvey's Market, The District Fish Wife seafood market and the Trickling Springs Creamery store.

Baltimore's Neopol Savory Smokery, which produces an astonishing array of smoked fish, meats, vegetables, and cheeses, does brisk business at Union Market and at its original location in Baltimore's Belvedere Square Market. This food emporium has been anchored by Atwater's Bakery, an early and stalwart supporter of local farms and producers, since 2003. Atwater's sells at many farmers markets in Baltimore and DC and sources ingredients for baked goods, soups, and salads from their farmers market buddies. HEX Ferments, a maker of traditionally fermented foods such as sauerkraut, kimchi, and kombucha, using local organic produce, is also based in Belvedere Square Market.

ping away at a mission to deliver fresh, organic, and local food to places where most consumers shop—supermarkets and co-ops" for twenty to thirty years. He acknowledged that it was counterintuitive at a time when the local food story was all about "bustling farmers markets, community-supported agriculture programs that deliver a box of vegetables to your door, or farmers hauling freshly butchered lamb into restaurants." But he insisted that "this work will need to be replicated many times over if fresh, local foods are going to reach customers beyond high-end restaurants and farmers markets, which represent two to three percent of food sales, and begin to show up on many more plates."

TOG, formed in 1988, was the go-to supplier of Certified Organic local produce for restaurants and stores that source local in 2008. They still supply scores of retailers in the Washington-Baltimore corridor and even supply some of the produce in the delivery boxes mentioned above. Pennsylvania is home to other large co-ops, including the Trickling Springs Creamery and Natural by Nature dairy cooperatives, plus the Lancaster Farm Fresh Cooperative mentioned previously. Local meat co-ops like Virginia's Shenandoah Valley Organics chicken and Shenandoah Valley Beef Cooperative are also examples of "middleman" organizations, helping a group of small farmers collectively move larger quantities of food from their farms to our plates.

Farmers growing all manner of field

greens, squashes, corn, peppers, green beans, melons, and more sell their food to the highest bidders at local produce auctions, such as the Loveville Produce Auction in Southern Maryland and the Shenandoah Valley Produce Auction in Virginia. Buyers from farm stands and stores that source local shop at these auctions, alongside buyers from regional and national grocery store chains. Farmers also sell through produce distributors like Coastal Sunbelt, Hearn Kirkwood, and Keany, who resell to restaurants, caterers, cafeterias and other foodservice companies. Both auctions and distributors push lots of local produce into the marketplace, but it loses its specific farm identity and story of how it's produced by the time it gets to the consumer. The local food movement is all about knowing where your food comes from, so farmers wanted a better way to sell wholesale without having their products become simply part of the commodity produce stream.

Food hubs respond to this need by serving as a central point for the storage, marketing, sale, and distribution of local sustainably grown produce (and sometimes other products) to stores, restaurants, and institutional foodservice buyers like hospitals, schools, and other facilities. The output of several farms may be aggregated to accommodate large buyers, but the food hub offers traceability and transparency, so buyers can know exactly where the food was produced.

Charlottesville's Local Food Hub, founded in 2009, has provided a model for the way a food hub can not only connect buyers with the local sustainable agriculture community but also be the venue for providing technical assistance to farmers on topics such as food safety and handling, which open new doors for a small farmer's products. Local Food Hub operates within an increasingly populated region of Central Virginia and has helped get local farmers' products into more local restaurants and stores, as well as into several school districts and certain foodservice operations at the University of Virginia.

The Common Market, based in Philadelphia (not to be confused with Common Market Co-Op in Frederick, Maryland) and one of the largest food hubs on the East Coast, works on a scale several times that of Local Food Hub, but its work is based on the same principles. Common Market believes it can change the way people eat at a systemic level by establishing local food conduits to anchor institutions, where thousands of people eat every day, such as Philadelphia's universities, schools, and healthcare facilities. While influencing public health indicators through broader access to healthy, fresh, sustainably produced food, Common Market also helps the region's farmers

The local producers' chalk board at Locke Modern Country Store in Millwood, Virginia.
Photo by Renee Brooks Catacalos.

enhance their own financial stability. "Food hubs are one of many new attractive markets that help solve distribution challenges" for local farmers, said Common Market's procurement director Andrew Puglia.

Even if they are able to pay a fair farm price for locally produced food, schools, hospitals, and other institutions often have food safety requirements, approved vendor restrictions, storage challenges, or other logistical issues that make direct sourcing from farms problematic. Food hubs and distributors that offer locally traceable products help overcome those obstacles.

Not every organization that aggregates food has "food hub" in its name. DC Central Kitchen is a nonprofit that operates social ventures aimed at breaking the cycles of poverty and homelessness. Among its many award-winning programs, DC Central Kitchen uses surplus and purchased food from local farms to provide nutritious, scratch-cooked meals to homeless shelters and nonprofit service providers, as well as to fifteen schools in low-income areas of the city.

Trust and Verify

Whenever anyone gets between you and the farm, whether it's a produce buyer or a restaurant chef or a cafeteria foodservice supervisor, there's the chance that something could get lost in the translation, namely the identity of a local farm or the verification that a farm cited is actually supplying the food claimed.

Look to the farm sources for help. If a restaurant says it sources from a particular farm, check that farm's website or give them call to ask if it's true. If an establishment says they purchase from a food hub or a co-op brand, check the food hub's information for verification. For instance, Chesapeake Farm to Table, a farmer-run food hub that connects more than twenty local farms with several dozen Baltimore-area customers, prominently lists on its website the restaurants, caterers, and retailers that buy from the hub. Many individual farms list their customers as well. You can cross-check that Liberty Delight Farms does sell to Union Hospital and that Sassafras Creek Farm does sell to Geppetto Catering by looking at those farms' lists of partners.

Similarly, you can use these resources to deliberately seek out the places that are buying from local farms and food hubs. Shenandoah Valley Organics chicken is identified by their packaging in stores, but their website has a locator to tell you where to find the group's products if you're not sure where to look. From the Liberty Delight website, I learned that I can get a locally sourced beef shawarma at Arba Mediterranean in Baltimore. You can also ask your favorite farmers directly, if you've heard they sell to a certain place and want to be sure, or if you want to know where to go to be sure you are eating their food. Farmers are very happy to share and to promote those businesses that truly support them!

Sausage and Summer Vegetable Skillet

I first made this dish using rosemary and garlic lamb sausage from Forrest Pritchard's Smith Meadows Farm in Berryville, Virginia, but any highly seasoned pork, beef, or lamb sausage will work. Choose a sausage that's bold enough to flavor the entire dish. The recipe is easily expandable and adaptable to whatever fresh vegetables happen to be on hand.

1 pound seasoned lamb or pork sausage
1 small onion, roughly chopped
1 cup homemade chicken or vegetable stock
2 cups corn, cut off the cob
1 medium yellow squash or zucchini, chopped into 1-inch pieces
2 tomatoes, roughly chopped
½ teaspoon salt
½ teaspoon black pepper

If using links, remove the casings and place the sausage and chopped onion in a large skillet. Sauté over medium-high heat for 4-5 minutes, until broken up and no longer pink. Add the rest of the ingredients, cover, and simmer for 10-15 minutes, stirring occasionally, until the squash is soft. Serve hot with rice, your favorite bread, and plain yogurt. Serves 4-6.

6 | Liquid Harvests

After leading the colonial forces to an improbable victory in the American Revolution and serving two terms as president of the new nation, George Washington retired to his plantation at Mount Vernon, Virginia, and became the nation's biggest whiskey manufacturer.

He didn't begin his distilling operation until he retired from public life in 1797, but by the time he died less than three years later, the distillery at Mount Vernon was producing nearly eleven thousand gallons of rye whiskey annually and was one of the most profitable enterprises on the sprawling plantation. Washington was the only founding father to go into the spirits business (Thomas Jefferson tried, but failed, to start the American wine industry) but not the only early American businessman who saw the potential for profit in alcohol. In 1810, there were thirty-six hundred distilleries in Virginia alone.

Touring the reconstructed distillery at Mount Vernon made me realize how little I knew about alcoholic beverages and their relationship to our local food community. When I learned that wherever there was a gristmill grinding grain, there was probably a distillery nearby in early America, I wondered why that had changed. I wondered what happened to the breweries of nineteenth-century moguls like Christian Heurich, whose magnificent Victorian mansion in Dupont Circle is still called "The Brewmaster's Castle." I asked myself how Virginia wine became such a bright light in the local food economy, more than two centuries after Jefferson's vineyard failures.

It turns out that Prohibition and its aftermath were responsible for the demise and long dormancy of local distilling and brewing but also contained the loophole that led to the birth of not only our local wine culture, but the American wine industry itself, right here in the mid-Atlantic. The modern craft beverage industry in general, and local farm-based alcohol businesses specifically, are still unraveling the effects of Prohibition through organized

Bartenders created cocktails using Maryland spirits at one of the Maryland Distillers Guild's tasting events in Baltimore. Photo by Tara Howell / Maryland Distillers Guild.

and proactive advocacy to change state and local rules around the production, sale, and distribution of alcoholic beverages that drastically favor large beverage corporations.

Prohibition

When the early settlers arrived on the shores of the Chesapeake, they had dreams of making wine. In fact, the Virginia expedition's investors made it mandatory for settlers to plant vineyards, in hopes of creating exportable wine and ending British dependence on wines from continental Europe. The Virginians found some native grapes and attempted to establish vineyards, but they quickly shifted their focus to the cash potential of the mildly intoxicating tobacco leaf, which the native people of the region cultivated for wide-ranging healing uses.

While wine-making dreams fell by the wayside, the distilling of spirits flourished. Prior to the Revolution, the colonists mainly distilled rum from molasses, imported from Caribbean plantations, where it was a by-product of sugar production. When the Revolution interrupted the Caribbean trade, the colonists began distilling whiskey from homegrown grains that were cheap and plentiful—corn, wheat, and rye. These spirits were clear and were distributed for drinking immediately, without aging. Farm families brewed ale or fermented apple cider from the country's early days, but the immigration of millions of Germans to the United States in the 1800s led to a boom in commercial brewing. "German Belt" cities including Washington, Baltimore, and Philadelphia were home to more than four thousand breweries by 1873.

Domestic violence and the destitution of families caused by alcohol abuse; the passage of a US income tax law which theoretically would replace alcohol tax revenues; and anti-German sentiment building up to and during World War I—these were among the factors contributing to the rapid adoption of the Eighteenth Amendment, prohibiting the manufacture, sale, and distribution of alcoholic beverages in 1920. The politically powerful temperance movement had already worked to decrease alcohol consumption from an all-time high of more than 7 gallons per person per year in 1830 to around 2 gallons by 1920. But Prohibition knocked the hard-drinking nation for a loop in many other ways: tens of thousands of jobs were lost when saloons, breweries, and other related businesses shut down; violence escalated as organized crime created underground markets for booze; more people turned to drinking hard liquor, which was easier to conceal and transport than beer or wine; thousands of people died drinking unregulated alcohol that was often tainted with toxic substances; federal, state, and local governments were unable to replace alcohol tax revenue with income taxes as the Great Depression deepened. "The noble experiment" of Prohibition was repealed in 1933.

The Wine Loophole

It had only been thirteen years, but the damage was done. The nation's landscape of hop yards and apple orchards, and of breweries and distilleries, had been leveled. But, surprisingly, the seeds for our local wine industry had been sown, thanks to one of the loopholes in the law. The personal *consumption* of alcohol was not banned by Prohibition and, importantly, neither was making wine at home for personal use. Wine grapes continued to be planted and vineyards did a brisk business selling grapes and wine-making kits, and interest in wine-making grew.

One particularly avid and capable DIY winemaker was Baltimore journalist Philip Wagner. He spent the 1920s experimenting with grape vines and root stocks and ultimately developed successful hybrids of European *vinifera* grapes that were resistant to the diseases and pests of the eastern United States, providing the climate hardiness that had eluded Jefferson centuries before. In 1933, just after the repeal of Prohibition, Wagner published *American Wines and How to Make Them*, the first book on wine-making to be written in English and a catalyst to the modern American wine industry. He and his wife Jocelyn opened Boordy Vineyards in Baltimore County in 1945 as the first commercial vineyard and winery in Maryland.

Fast-forward to 2018, and Boordy Vineyards now produces one-third of the output of Maryland wineries, under the management of the DeFord family, which took over the operation in 1980, after growing grapes for the winery for the previous fifteen years. Although the vineyard was completely replanted in 2013 to take advantage of new research about vine spacing and vineyard management, the hybrid vines developed and sold by Philip Wagner from Boordy seeded the handful of vineyards that started the local wine movement in the 1960s and '70s. Six wineries opened in Virginia in the 1970s, slowly increasing to forty-six by 1995. The industry took off in the early 2000s, and today Virginia ranks sixth in the country, with 270 wineries at the end of 2017. In 2000, Maryland still had only forty wineries, but today that has doubled to more than seventy-five.

Virginia wine blogger Warren Richard carefully snips grapes during the fall harvest at Gray Ghost Vineyards. Photo by Paul Armstrong.

Farm Roots

It took much longer than the colonists or Thomas Jefferson projected, but wine is now the foundation of the Chesapeake region's farm-to-glass sector. The continuing cultivation of vineyards through Prohibition gave the wine industry a head start on reviving itself after Prohibition ended. By contrast, the agricultural base of other alcoholic beverages had all but been destroyed. The only commercial use for hops is for flavoring and preserving beer, so the cultivation of hops was abandoned. Apple orchards and backyard trees that could be used to produce hard cider had been ripped out. Grain harvests had been diverted to the war effort and suffered during the Great Depression.

But even winemakers had to contend with the federal government's new three-tiered alcohol distribution model, imposed in an attempt to forestall an immediate return to pre-Prohibition levels of inebriation. The three-tiered system required beverage producers to use a licensed distributor as a middleman between them and any retail outlets or end-use consumers, creating intentional logjams to slow the flow of alcohol back into society and preventing vertical monopolies on the production, distribution, and sale of alcohol. It also gave cash-strapped Depression-era governments the opportunity to tax the process at every step along the way, should they so choose. (Prohibition was no longer federal law, but state and local jurisdictions could maintain their own restrictions. Damascus, the last dry community in Maryland, lifted its prohibition in 2013. Smith Island, Maryland, does not have its own government to make separate regulations, but by tradition and practice, the community is dry. There are still ten dry counties in Virginia, but no dry cities, even if they are in a dry county.)

In practice, the three-tiered system also led to consolidation of alcohol production in large corporations and gave distributors the power to keep small producers out of the market. For local vineyards in the 1980s, distribution barriers included the ability to produce enough wine to satisfy a distributor's orders and the associated costs that had to be paid to the distributor. Small-volume wines are already more expensive to produce, and adding the distributor's markup along with the retail or restaurant markup meant that for consumers, local wines could not be cost competitive with larger brands.

Things changed when local vineyards asserted their right to pursue wine-making as an agricultural enterprise that adds value to the grapes grown in the vineyard. Through years of educating lawmakers and the public, they differentiated themselves from the alcohol production industry, in the same way that local food producers were differentiating themselves from industrial food producers. They made a successful case that their status as local farms should afford exemptions from the three-tiered alcohol distribution system.

Gaining the right to sell wine, beer, and spirits directly to consumers without going through a distributor opened many doors for the farm wineries, farm breweries, and farm distilleries in both Maryland and Virginia. They continue to lobby every year for additional opportunities to expand their businesses and serve consumers who want a great local beverage to go with their great local meal. Over the years, they've worked to change rules that limit the volume of beverages they can produce and sell, the locations and manner in which they can sell to consumers, how they can participate in special events like farmers markets and festivals, and whether they can self-distribute their products directly to retail outlets as well as to consumers.

These gains incentivize the continued use of farmland for these high-value agricultural uses. They have also created an increasing regional demand for growers to provide the raw agricultural inputs needed for alcoholic production—grapes, apples, honey, hops, and grains.

Lighter Libations

Local farm products turn up in nonalcoholic drinkable forms as well. Some are meant to be mixed into adult beverages, like local tomatoes and peppers in Bloody Mary mixes. Fruits and herbs form the base for shrubs, old-fashioned syrups made sharp with vinegar and mixed with carbonated water for sodas or with alcohol for cocktails.

Many local farms offer herbal teas, which are technically tisanes since they do not contain tea. Only the leaves and buds of the *Camellia sinensis* bush, a subtropical plant, are truly tea. The closest thing to local tea currently available is green tea from Charleston Tea Plantation in South Carolina, which is available in some stores and online.

I mentioned fresh cider before, and I'd have to say that this may be one good thing that came from Prohibition. Unfiltered cider is like drinking an apple in a glass. Very few farmers bring unpasteurized cider to farmers markets anymore, but you can still find it at some farm stands, including Heyser Farms in Silver Spring, Maryland. I make a point to buy an extra half gallon or two near the end of the cider season, pour a little out to drink, then freeze the rest. It thaws perfectly for a welcome winter treat.

Kombucha, a nonalcoholic fermented drink made with tea and probiotic cultures, is very popular these days and offered by many local farms and makers. It can be flavored with local, seasonal ingredients. The Sweet Farm in Frederick, Maryland, offers a unique fermented ginger beer, for sale in growlers on tap at Common Market in Frederick. Local dairies also sell a wide range of milk and milk-based drinks, including flavored milks, yogurt drinks, and kefirs.

Grapes

Research and experimentation have made it possible for vintners to successfully grow *vinifera* varieties of grapes in Maryland and Virginia. *Vinifera* grapes include the varieties most wine drinkers are familiar with—Cabernet Franc, Chardonnay, Merlot, Cabernet Sauvignon, and Petit Verdot lead the list of local plantings, with significant plantings in Virginia of Viognier, the first *vinifera* variety that really flourished in our climate and produced quality wines. *Vinifera* grapes generate more revenue per acre for vineyards and more revenue per bottle for vintners because wine drinkers will pay more for the types of wines they are used to seeing from Europe and California.

In fact, *vinifera* make up the majority of local vines. But many hybrids continue to be popular. These grapes have less familiar names, such as Chambourcin, Vidal Blanc, Seyval Blanc, and Traminette. Hybrids produce higher grape yields per acre but at a lower profit than *vinifera* grapes. But hybrids offer other advantages. Certain fungal diseases that affect *vinifera* grapes in the Chesapeake region have no organic treatments, making it impossible for vineyards to achieve organic certification. Many wineries use farming practices as close to organic as they can, but there is so far only one Certified Organic vineyard in the region, Virginia's Loving Cup Vineyard and Winery. They've achieved this is by ditching the *vinifera* varieties altogether and growing only disease-resistant hybrids such as Traminette and Cayuga, a white grape they describe as "the variety we think is most compatible with organic production in Virginia."

There is also a small but vocal fan club for Norton, a hybrid developed in Virginia in the early 1800s and included in Slow Food USA's "Ark of Taste" catalog of distinctive and endangered foods as "the oldest cultivated American grape." Virginia vintners Dennis Horton of Horton Vineyards in Gordonsville and Jenni McCloud of Chrysalis Vineyards in Middleburg each produce a variety of lovely wines using many different grapes. They have also been the leading advocates for the Norton grape, promoting its ability to produce better wine than native grapes such as Concord or Niagara. Horton calls Norton wine "the original Virginia claret."

The Norton grape has been more divisive than it seems that a grape should be. In my mind, if you like it, drink it, and if you don't like it, leave those who do alone. But the Norton grape has sparked quite a number of debates and small controversies, many of which former *Washingtonian* food editor Todd Kliman details in his 2011 book, *The Wild Vine*. I'm not a wine expert, but I appreciate fullness and character in a glass of red wine. I like a wine that reminds you that it is an integral and distinctive part of your meal and not just a chaser for your food. I have enjoyed the Horton and Chrysalis Nortons and think it's exciting to see more wineries including Norton in their offerings. McCloud is such an evangelist for this grape that the Chrysalis website includes a listing of more than forty producers of Norton wines, primarily in Virginia and Missouri, where Norton was preserved during the time it fell out of favor on the East Coast. Virginia winemakers are using Norton to make more than just claret, such as Keswick Vineyards Amelie Rose, a sparkling wine made with Norton grapes.

Most of the region's wineries are also vineyards growing their own grapes, but there are some wineries that have no grape production of their own.

Winery owner and winemaker Katie DeSouza pours for my sister Stacy and me at Casanel Vineyards when we visited with wine bloggers Warren Richard and Paul Armstrong. Photo by Paul Armstrong.

Even wineries with vineyards sometimes source grapes from other growers, either for the sake of a particular blend, to make up for harvest shortfalls, or because they just don't have the room to grow as many grapes as they need to keep up with the wine-making demand. Both Virginia and Maryland experience ongoing in-state grape shortages, so wineries are allowed to source a certain percentage of grapes from out of state. However, the acreage planted in wine grapes is steadily increasing to try to meet the demand of winemakers.

The Maryland Grape Grower's Association's 2014 vineyard census showed that over 61 percent of the grapes used in Maryland wine were grown in Maryland, up from 53 percent in 2010. The Virginia Wine Board meanwhile has issued a vision statement that foresees an increase in the amount of vineyard production to meet 100 percent of the demand from Virginia farm wineries by 2020.

Before Prohibition, cider always referred to a fermented alcoholic drink, made using the same process as wine but from fruit other than grapes. It was during Prohibition that fresh, or unfermented, apple cider became common, leading to today's usage of "hard" cider to mean alcoholic cider.

Apples were and still are the most common cider fruit, but you might see pear, plum, or peach cider as well. Johnny Appleseed, portrayed in school books as an agricultural Santa gifting American pioneers with apple trees, was not supplying them with an apple a day to keep the doctor away as much as the raw ingredients for hard cider, which might have been an equally valuable guarantor of good health on the hardscrabble frontier. Cider was most commonly pressed and fermented at home rather than as a commercial enterprise. On occasion, I've left fresh, unpasteurized apple cider in the fridge a few days too long and made my own hard cider without even trying.

But my fizzed-up refrigerator cider is a far cry from the products coming out of the thirty or so cideries across Maryland and Virginia. Orchards specializing in heritage apples, including the tart, acidic apples that used to be prized for making cider, led the way in creating today's cider culture. Foggy Ridge in southwestern Virginia was the first modern cidery in Virginia when it opened in 2005, an expansion of the heirloom orchard of the same name. (The owners of Foggy Ridge stopped making cider in 2018 to refocus on their original business of growing heirloom cider apples.) Vintage Virginia Apples is another heirloom apple orchard that went into cider-making as Albemarle Ciderworks.

While I was working at Future Harvest–CASA, we organized educational field days for farmers to visit some of Maryland's first modern cider makers, including Distillery Lane Ciderworks in Jefferson and Country Pleasures Farm in Middletown, the first organic orchard in Maryland, now producing cider using organic apples under the label Willow Oaks Craft Cider.

Pennsylvania, Maryland, Virginia, and West Virginia are all apple-growing states, with plenty of old orchards to supply the current stock of cideries and many more. Ciders are not made from the same apples we eat but from crabapples and species with colorful names such as Hewes Crab, Albemarle Pippin, Winesap, and Roxbury Russet. These are not apples you would want to bite into fresh, just as wine grapes are not recommended for the table. But their versatility allows them to be blended into beverages ranging from very

Virginia's wineries and cideries use heirloom apples and other local ingredients to make a variety of ciders, from sweet to dry. Photo courtesy of Virginia Association of Cider Makers.

sweet to dry and refined, with descriptions akin to wine notes, complete with food pairings.

Cider can be left unfiltered and with a bit of carbonation or it can be filtered, which makes it clearer and less fizzy. It can be aged in barrels, like wine, to add complex flavors. Some cider makers add additional herbs, other fruits, or hops to create interesting, modern ciders for just about every taste.

Honey can also be fermented and is widely understood to have been the first food fermented into an alcoholic drink, mead. It was never as popular in America as it had been in Europe, and even in Europe its heyday was the Middle Ages. But mead is now a fast-growing segment of the craft beverage industry, with nearly five hundred mead producers around the country, including about thirty across Maryland and Virginia. While medieval-esque meads are certainly available, modern meads can be light and refreshing, with a variety of flavor profiles. Some meads have alcohol content equal to wines, but others—particularly those bottled before fermentation is complete so they retain their carbonation—are in the alcohol range of beers and ciders.

Meadmakers may top off their recipes with some local honey, but the demand for honey already far outpaces local supply. In 2017, Andrew Geffken at

Raw Milk—The New Moonshine

The US Food and Drug Administration (FDA) has banned the interstate sale and distribution of raw, or unpasteurized, milk. But states make their own rules regarding how raw milk is handled within their borders, and those rules vary wildly. The production and consumption of raw milk is not generally regulated, only the ability of farmers to sell that milk to consumers.

Until 2006, both Maryland and Virginia prohibited the sale of raw milk for human consumption but allowed arrangements called cow shares or herd shares. Cow shares allow consumers to buy a "share" of a cow, so they are technically drinking raw milk from their own cow, which is legal under state laws, rather than buying raw milk from the farmer, which is illegal. Dozens of farms offer cow shares and goat shares in Virginia today.

But in 2006, the Maryland Department of Health and Mental Hygiene banned cow shares. In the meantime, over the border in Pennsylvania, where raw milk could be sold anywhere but required a license and certain equipment based on high-volume milk production, small dairy farmers created a consumer buyers club. They argued that the direct relationship between farmers and consumers was not the same as retail and exempted them from the licensing requirements, which they felt were cost prohibitive and out of line for small operations like theirs.

Maryland mom and activist Liz Reitzig helped Maryland consumers connect with these Pennsylvania farmers to buy raw milk and other farm products. I had known her for more than a year before she trusted me enough to add me to the email list for her Grassfed on the Hill buyers club. There was never any chance that I was going to be fined or arrested for buying the Pennsylvania raw milk. But the danger to the farmers supplying it was real, and hence the secrecy and vetting of new customers.

Buying contraband raw milk did make me feel like I was making an important statement, exercising my right to choose the food I wanted for myself and my family, based on my own understanding of the safety and risks of my choice, a choice that did not compel anyone else to drink raw milk if they didn't want to. My kids reveled in the hint of spy-novel intrigue involved in going to the "secret" drop points to pick up the creamy milk that tasted slightly sweet and in some way more complete than what we were used to drinking.

The cloak-and-dagger moves turned out to have been warranted when the US Food and Drug Administration (which, maybe not incidentally, moved its national headquarters to Maryland around the same time) did, in fact, infiltrate the club with undercover agents. They staged pre-dawn raids on the Amish farm supplying our club and pursued aggressive legal action against the farmer, Dan Allgyer. After two years of being harried by the FDA, Allgyer shut down his farm altogether.

Maryland advocates continued to push and, in 2015, the Maryland Department of Agriculture (MDA), which has jurisdiction over animal health, approved the sale of raw milk for consumption by pets. I doubt anyone is under the impression that four-legged consumers are drinking the bulk of the "raw pet milk" now sold in the state. Advocates would still like to see the ban on human consumption officially lifted, but the new MDA rule puts Maryland in the category of the more than forty states that allow sales of raw milk, according to the Weston A. Price Foundation, a leading lobbying and education organization for raw milk.

With moonshine now respectable and cannabis legalization on the horizon, how long can it make sense for regulators to keep fighting a small number of citizens, who fully understand the potential health risks, who just want to buy milk straight from the cow?

Charm City Meadworks told me, "We use local fruit and herbs when we can," as well as a few hundred pounds of local honey for special offerings, but he doesn't see the capacity within the local beekeeping industry to keep up with the growth of meaderies. "This year," he said, "we expect to use more honey than the entire state of Maryland produces."

Hops

Hops, the flowers of a plant in the cannabis family, grow on long, climbing bines (bines climb by twining around their support, whereas vines climb with the aid of tendrils) that require special trellising and harvesting equipment. It was once common for farmers to grow hops for their own beer-making, and beer-making was a commonly held skill in farm families. Since the only real use for the hop plant is its ability to impart flavor-enhancing bitterness and preservative antibacterial properties to beer, when Prohibition eliminated that need, the cultivation of hops here and across the country fell into decline.

After Prohibition, the Pacific Northwest became the center of American hops growing. Hops can be shipped as dried flowers or as concentrated pellets, and most hobby brewers order them from Washington, Oregon, and Idaho. Barley malt and other grains, as well as brewer's yeast, can be more easily shipped for beer-making than grapes can for wine-making. Perhaps owing to this portability, as well as the more complicated process involved in brewing beer, craft brewing in our area launched with less emphasis on using local ingredients.

Tom Barse of Stillpoint Farm in Mount Airy, Maryland, opened Milkhouse Brewery in 2013 and helped draft the legislation that established the state's farm brewery license. His Chinook hops are harvested using a piece of equipment he built himself that spools the long bines and strips off the sticky flowers. Milkhouse was the first farm brewery in Maryland, but there

Corn is transformed into smooth bourbon on the same farm where it's grown at Tobacco Barn Distillery in Southern Maryland. Photo by Tobacco Barn Distillery.

are now at least ten farmhouse breweries throughout the state and about an equal number in Virginia. They are sometimes connected to existing produce and grain farms, like Milkhouse, and sometimes an offshoot of a winery.

Even with the limited amounts of beer allowed to be sold under the farm brewery license, it will be years before these farms can produce enough hops for all their own needs. Maryland farmers grew a mere 15 acres of hops in 2015, the first year there was enough to record statistically. By contrast, Washington State, which produces 70 percent of the country's hops, grew more than thirty-two thousand acres that year. Both Maryland and Virginia are working to help farmers who want to grow local hops, either for their own farm breweries or for sale to local brewers. Luckettsville Hops Works at Black Hops Farm in Loudoun County, Virginia, and Black Locust Hops in Baltimore County are among the enterprises seeking to stake a claim for commercial hops producers in the region. They have planted acres of hops for sale to local brewers and are also working to process dried pelletized hops. One brewer at a Maryland beer tasting event whispered to me, "Don't start a brewery, the money now is in hops!"

Grains

The other key ingredient for beer is malted barley—grain that has been moistened, allowed to sprout, and then dried, which gives it a nutty, sweet flavor and makes its starches more readily available for fermenting into alcohol. Some farm breweries grow and malt their own barley. But a new agricultural niche has opened up for farmers to grow barley specifically to sell to breweries or to malting facilities now under development in our region.

Grain-to-glass distillers are working with local corn, rye, and other grains, as well as fruits, herbs, honeys, and spring water to create their local liquors. Tobacco Barn Distillery in Southern Maryland uses its own corn and spring water, plus molasses from the Domino Sugar processing plant in Baltimore, to craft its rum. Virginia's Belmont Farm Distillery crafts a vodka from corn as well as corn moonshine. McClintock Distilling Company out of Frederick, Maryland, flavors its Forager Gin with native botanicals harvested in the nearby Appalachian hills. Bloomery Plantation Distillery has the distinction of making award-winning limoncello using lemons grown in their own fantastic greenhouse—in Charles Town, West Virginia!

Eggnog

Ever since the Brits set foot in Jamestown, some version of a milk-and-egg punch flavored with rum or other spirits has been part of the American winter holiday experience. In my family, my grandmother's eggnog made its first appearance at Thanksgiving—purchased from the grocery store but "fortified" with her triple-threat blend of rum, bourbon, and brandy and smoothed by the folding in of a generous amount of freshly whipped cream. The tradition continues at my mom's house, where we check the fridge for eggnog every time we stop by, all the way through New Year's.

You can buy delicious eggnog from local dairies, but it's a treat to make and taste old-fashioned eggnog. This creamy delight is a lovely combination of fresh eggs, dairy, and spirits, all of which can be from your favorite local producers. This recipe uses the ratio of ¼ cup alcohol for each egg yolk recommended by the Food Network's food scientist Alton Brown. Alcohol can't be guaranteed to kill all bacteria that might be present, but the risk here is pretty slim. Feel free to vary the alcohol you use based on your own preferences, but keep to the ratio for safety with the raw eggs. You want to make sure you can actually taste the alcohol flavors.

6 large eggs
1½ cups confectioner's sugar
1 teaspoon nutmeg, freshly grated if possible
1 cup half-and-half
1 cup milk
2 cups heavy whipping cream, divided
½ cup brandy
½ cup dark rum
½ cup bourbon
Pinch of kosher salt

Separate the eggs. Store the whites for another purpose, such as making meringues. Place the yolks in a large mixing bowl and whisk them with the sugar and nutmeg until the mixture lightens in color and streams off the whisk in a smooth ribbon, about 3 or 4 minutes.

Combine the half-and-half, milk, and 1 cup of heavy cream with the alcohol and salt in a separate bowl. Slowly whisk this dairy-booze mixture into the egg mixture.

Whip the remaining 1 cup of heavy cream to soft peaks. Ladle about a cup of the eggnog into the bowl and fold it into the whipped cream until smooth, then fold the entire cream mixture back into the eggnog bowl.

Transfer to a large pitcher or jar and chill. A little freshly grated nutmeg on each cup when serving is a nice flourish.

Makes 2 quarts.

7 | Building a Local Food System

After a decade of progress, the local food system faces some serious questions about how it continues to grow and mature. Can local farmers achieve financial sustainability while simultaneously expanding access and affordability for consumers? Can we keep the local food system from devolving to include the same patterns of racial, social, economic, and geographic inequity that we are fighting in the industrial food system? Does a local food economy that accounts for 1 or 2 percent of the food consumed in our region have even the slightest systemic impact?

Very few people believe we are going to completely replace the broken global food system. But the momentum achieved by local and regional food systems across the country makes a strong case for believing that some of the damage can be repaired, and some parts of the system can be replaced with better alternatives. One thing is clear: our local food system MUST create more opportunities for all the people, voices, cultures, creatures, farms, food, and businesses that inhabit the Chesapeake region, in order to reach the critical mass that begins to change the way the larger food system works.

Part of the challenge, and perhaps one of the reasons our prevailing food system doesn't work, is that the responsibility and authority for making policy that affects food up and down production, sales, and distribution chains is spread across too many different government agencies and departments. The United States does not have a "secretary for food" or any single office that oversees the food system in its entirety, leading to inconsistencies at the national level. These become compounded by inconsistencies among federal, state, and local jurisdictions.

At least seventeen different federal agencies make rules and policies that impact the food system, generally without reference to or knowledge of policies of other agencies that might be contradictory. The Blueprint for a National Food Strategy published by food systems researchers at Vermont Law School and Harvard Law School summarizes the stunning disconnects that result. For example, the introduction of the Food Safety and Modernization Act (FSMA) by the Food and Drug Administration in 2011 created an uproar over the blanket application of the regulations to large food corporations whose produce ingredients pass through a long supply chain before reaching the consumer and also to small produce farms seeking to serve local customers directly or with a very short supply chain. This happened as the US Department of Agriculture (USDA) was simultaneously offering small farmers a variety of grant programs, technical assistance, and marketing support to help them connect with local consumers. The FSMA regulations were ultimately revised to better accommodate small and medium-sized farmers serving local food communities.

In another example, federal dietary and nutrition guidelines issued jointly by the USDA and the US Department of Health and Human Services emphasize consumption of fruits and vegetables as the top two components of a healthy diet. At the same time, most federal agricultural subsidies go to commodity crops such as corn and soybeans, which are used in industrial meat production and in the manufacture of highly processed food, both of which the nutrition guidelines recommend we should minimize or avoid.

Those commodity crop subsidies are included in the piece of federal legislation most directly connected with food, commonly known as the Farm Bill. A new Farm Bill is supposed to be passed by Congress every five years, but the process is often delayed, resulting in short-term extensions that keep permanently funded programs running while lawmakers work to finalize a comprehensive bill. The current Farm Bill, officially called the Agricultural Act of 2014, followed the Food, Conservation and Energy Act of 2008, which expired in 2012. When the 2008 bill expired, USDA programs with permanent funding continued at their previously appropriated levels until a new bill could be voted into law. But many of the programs that support local and sustainable practices did not and still do not have permanent funding. During the 2013 extension, funding of the Farmers Market Promotion Program temporarily ceased and no grants were awarded until the following year.

Local Effects of Farm Bill Programs

The fraction of Farm Bill programs that are targeted to local and regional food systems have had a catalyzing effect here in the Chesapeake region, attracting additional state and foundation funding to many of the building blocks of the local food economy.

Beginning Farmer and Rancher Development Program

Funding from this Farm Bill program has helped Future Harvest –CASA train nearly 170 new farmers through its Beginner Farmer Training Program. ECO City Farms has used its grant funding to focus on training urban farmers, as well as minority and new immigrant farmers, in conjunction with Prince George's Community College and other partners. Arcadia Center for Sustainable Food and Agriculture in Virginia has used program funds to work with veterans who want to farm, offering training, apprenticeships, and assistance in finding land.

Farmers Market Promotion Program

Since 2006, this program has fueled the expansion of farmers markets in rural, suburban, and urban communities across the Chesapeake region. Funds have been used for start-up costs for new markets, especially in economically disadvantaged locations, marketing and advertising programs to increase farmers market sales, purchase of equipment for processing of SNAP (Supplemental Nutrition Assistance Program) benefits at farmers markets, technical assistance to help farmers with safe food handling and effective market displays, and other strategies to support the sales of local agricultural products through farmers markets.

Local Food Promotion Program

Focusing on local food strategies beyond farmers markets, this program has helped fund the development of technology and infrastructure for food hubs, meat processing facilities for local livestock farmers, mobile farmers markets to reach food deserts in Baltimore and DC, business incubators for local food enterprises, and other projects that either expand or create new local supply chain opportunities for agricultural producers.

Value-Added Producer Grants

The Farm Bill also includes a program that helps farmers create value-added agricultural products. These have included numerous wine, beer, and spirits operations, production of farmstead cheeses and locally raised meats, processing and packaging of local oysters, and establishment or expansion of community-supported agriculture (CSA) programs.

The Agricultural Act of 2014 is set to expire on September 30, 2018. Advocates for sustainable local food systems are pushing for a new Farm Bill to be enacted on time and for permanent funding of the programs that have been so critical to local food economies. It's not only possible, it's highly probable that this effort will still be under way by the time this book is published. The National Sustainable Agriculture Coalition (NSAC) is the leading voice on Capitol Hill lobbying for policies and funding that support sustainable agriculture and local food issues in the Farm Bill and other federal legislation. The Chesapeake Bay Foundation, Virginia Association for Biological Farming, Johns Hopkins University Center for a Livable Future, Future Harvest–CASA, The Common Market (PA), Pennsylvania Association for Sustainable Agriculture, and the West Virginia Food and Farm Coalition are among the one hundred grassroots organizations collaborating under the NSAC banner. Check their website, sustainableagriculture.net, for excellent background resources, legislative updates, and opportunities to take action to support sustainable agriculture and local food systems priorities in the Farm Bill.

The Farm Bill and Hunger

What is actually in the Farm Bill often surprises people as much as what's not. The bulk of Farm Bill funding, around 80 percent, goes to anti-hunger programs, primarily the Supplemental Nutrition Assistance Program (SNAP). Long known as the food stamp program, SNAP is the current incarnation of government attempts, going back to the 1930s, to address both food insecurity among the population and surplus food production by farmers. The SNAP program is a perennial target for lawmakers seeking to scale back spending, but supporters point to the program's effectiveness as a responsive tool for combating hunger during tough economic times. When unemployment is lower and the economy is doing well, participation in the program decreases. The USDA reports that a record-high 47.6 million participants redeemed $76 million in SNAP benefits in fiscal year 2013. As the economy has improved, those numbers have steadily decreased, dropping to just over $58 billion in benefits redeemed by 42.1 million participants in fiscal year 2017.

However, health and anti-hunger advocates warn against reducing funding levels to be prepared for future downturns. The program also offers emergency assistance when disasters strike, even in strong economic times. For instance, while SNAP redemptions dropped significantly across the country

Washington, DC, residents organized by DC Greens, a nonprofit that promotes collaborations to support food education, food access, and food policy, advocate for funding of the Produce Plus farmers market program.
Photo by Lillie Rosen and Dominique Hazzard, courtesy of DC Greens.

in fiscal year 2017, both Texas and Florida saw sharp increases in participation following the devastation of Hurricanes Harvey and Irma.

The funds allocated to SNAP recipients are pumped back into the economy as food purchases. When incentives are provided for using SNAP benefits to purchase directly from farmers, those federal dollars go directly into our local food system. Ironically, the income of many farmers (and others working in the food system) qualifies them for SNAP as well, though their participation rates have been shown to be lower than that for non-farm families.

The Farm Bill and Agriculture

After SNAP, the remaining 20 percent of the Farm Bill deals directly with agriculture: roughly 9 percent for crop insurance subsidies, 6 percent for conservation programs, and 5 percent for subsidies to growers of commodities—corn, wheat, and soybeans. *The remaining 1 percent of funding in the Farm Bill contains almost all the programs that have helped expand the local food movement since 1996.*

NSAC and others working for local and sustainable food systems will be advocating to improve the conservation and crop insurance portions of the Farm Bill by removing barriers to eligibility for sustainable farming practices and ensuring that the programs equitably serve farms of all types, sizes, and geography. But a large part of their efforts are aimed at preserving funding for SNAP and the "1 percent" of programs directly targeted at local and sustainable food systems.

A larger portion of the budget pie might seem warranted to those of us who care about local and sustainable food, but that 1 percent has arguably had a more far-reaching impact than the dollar value would suggest. A tiny investment has served as seed money to spur additional spending and collaborations from state and local governments, as well as private foundations and organizations.

The Farm Bill may be the most comprehensive single piece of legislation affecting farmers, but it is not the only one. Other specific issues might be taken up by congressional agriculture committees between Farm Bills. In addition, many other issues that affect farming are not within the purview of the agriculture committees, including farm worker and food worker rights, US Food and Drug Administration–controlled food safety issues, clean water and renewable fuels, public lands and grazing rights, and fisheries.

State Food Policy

Some federal policies, such as the FSMA, set regulations that must be adhered to by farmers at the local level. Other policies establish incentives to promote certain practices or address certain production gaps. These include the local food programs in the Farm Bill, as well as its contradictory commodity subsidies. Some incentive programs are administered directly by the federal government, while others are shunted down to the state level, where the bulk of farming operations are regulated. Just as at the federal level, multiple agencies can be involved, primarily those related to agriculture, health and nutrition, natural and marine resources, and alcoholic beverages.

State block grants from the USDA for promoting the production of "specialty crops," meaning fruits and vegetables, nuts, flowers, and other crops that are not considered commodities, are awarded and administered through a competitive grant process by each state agriculture department. Agriculture departments in our region regulate farm production, processing of farm products, marketing, and licensing, as well as farmers markets. They also play an important role in promoting local foods through their branded marketing programs, such as Virginia Grown and Maryland's Best. State programs can help farmers and food producers qualify for federal grants by providing required matching funds and loans. States also signal policy priorities through their allocation of funding to agricultural research.

The Senior Farmers Market Nutrition Program is also authorized through the Farm Bill and block-granted to states. However, the Women, Infants, and Children (WIC) Farmers Market Nutrition Program and WIC Fruit and Vegetable Check program, both of which provide additional money that can be used at farmers markets, are funded through the Child Nutrition Act, a piece of legislation that also funds school food programs and requires reauthorization every five years like the Farm Bill. WIC programs are usually administered through a state's health department, but the WIC farmers market programs may be under the agriculture department or department of aging or elsewhere. Meanwhile, SNAP may be in a completely different agency charged with providing social services.

Not only is this confusing for consumers who use these benefits, it's also confusing for farmers and markets that want to accept them. One example of policy change to address this is the collaboration between the Maryland Department of Health and Mental Hygiene and the Maryland Department of Agriculture on joint trainings and streamlined applications for farmers accepting benefits administered by the respective agencies.

Maryland, Virginia, and DC support the creation of small food businesses through cottage food laws that relax or eliminate licensing requirements for certain types of baked and preserved foods offered for sale at farmers markets. This has also allowed farmers markets to offer a more diverse mix of foods to shoppers. As we saw in the last chapter, states exert a lot of control over farm-based alcohol production. That extends to limiting the number of farmers markets and special events a winery, brewery, or distillery may participate in each year. Farm-based beverage producers have achieved significant expansion by working with legislators to change the state policies that make it more difficult for them to be financially viable at a small scale.

Local Food Policy and Food Policy Councils

Until recently, policy makers in cities and counties had limited realization of how their local actions were affecting food access and resources. In some of our region's agricultural areas, zoning rules meant to preserve family farm-

Stakeholders work with facilitators from Johns Hopkins University's Food Policy Networks project during the formation of the Western Maryland Food Council. Photo by Cheryl DeBerry.

land from development could also stand in the way of letting unrelated beginning farmers access land. Agricultural activities such as beekeeping and housing backyard chickens were zoned out of most residential areas, as were many gardening activities on publicly visible lawns, putting those means of food production further away from people who could use them. Transportation decisions about where to build roads or put parking lots could isolate neighborhoods, discourage grocery stores and other food businesses, and lead to the creation of food deserts, disproportionately impacting people of color and low-income communities.

As federal and state policies began to catalyze local food systems work, the real-world effects of local policies, as well as potential conflicts between local policies and those trickling down from the state and federal levels, became more apparent. Local groups and governments scrambled to adapt and increasingly recognized that building regional and local food systems on the fly may not get us where we want to be in the long term. This has given birth to collaborations and deliberate efforts to map out food systems visions for the future, find opportunities to make positive changes before conflicts arise, and enable positive food systems growth with sensible and cohesive policies.

A lot of this work is being advanced through food policy councils, collaborations of stakeholders from all parts of the food system in a specific geographic area. This may include farmers and fishers, food producers, beverage makers, farmers market managers, food justice activists, nutritionists, food retailers, chefs and restaurateurs, food educators, food waste specialists, distributors, government planners, and others who work or volunteer in the food system, as well as local consumers.

According to the Food Policy Networks resource of Johns Hopkins University Center for a Livable Future, there are more than three hundred food policy councils nationwide. Food policy councils may be housed within government, be a partner of government, or be completely outside of it. They operate on the scale of cities, counties, regions, states, and multi-state regions.

There is no set format for how a food policy council should be structured, nor does every council address the same sorts of issues. But a common objective is to foster collaboration among participants in all parts of the food system, as a way to review, improve, streamline, and create policies that accurately reflect and evolve with a community's food values. Healthy food access is the top priority of the majority of food policy councils nationally, followed by economic development, land use/planning, food procurement, hunger relief, food production, food waste and recovery, food labor, and environmental issues.

Food policy councils often begin their work with food systems assessments, resource inventories, and gap analyses of the local food environment. This research helps them to prioritize the most pressing needs in the community and develop recommendations for solutions. This could result in the creation of a community-wide food plan or other guidance to ensure the inclusion of food issues during future zoning rewrites, sustainability planning, and comprehensive plan development.

They may then undertake a variety of activities that support or lead up to actual policy changes. Publishing a local food guide or organizing a local farm tour can help to raise awareness of food resources with both consumers and lawmakers. Producer-buyer conferences, presentations on finding land to farm, and projects that help fund shared resources, such as refrigerated storage or farm equipment, help advance economic development priorities. Technology resources and person-to-person relationships built through food policy councils can help expand networks for food recovery, donation, and composting.

The Fresh Beets pop-up market at Avenue Market in Baltimore is a project of the No Boundaries Coalition to bring fresh, healthy food to the Sandtown-Winchester area of West Baltimore. Photo by Brittany Britto for Capital News Service, University of Maryland College of Journalism.

A Food Policy Model: Baltimore Food Policy Initiative

The Sustainable Cities Initiative says: "BFPI [Baltimore Food Policy Initiative] demonstrates the impact cities can have on increasing food access through a strong policy approach—either by identifying and removing policy barriers or developing new policies that facilitate and encourage best practices." Launched in 2009, BFPI put Baltimore at the leading edge of food policy across the country. One of its key elements was the establishment of the position of Food Policy Director in the Department of Planning, one of the first "food czar" positions in the country.

"Wherever city money touches food, I should be watching it," says Holly Freishtat, who has held the position since 2010. The city pursues a "food in all policies" approach, with Freishtat as the link between the surprising range of departments with a role to play in some part of the food system—from the health department and the administrators of public markets to the labor commissioner's office, the transportation agencies, and emergency management authorities.

For example, to make it easier for urban farmers to start growing and selling produce in areas of low food access, coordination was required between departments regulating land use, water access, soil health, and infrastructure related to converting vacant land into agricultural production. A key change was eliminating the need for a permit before constructing a hoop house. In 2010, Real Food Farm, backed by the Baltimore Mayor's Office, the Baltimore nonprofit Civic Works, and a number of other funders and partners, launched the first urban hoop house farm in Baltimore, in Clifton Park. With 8 acres on two lots, Real Food Farm is one of the largest urban farms in the nation, according to the website SeedStock.com.

Today there are close to twenty urban farms in Baltimore operating neighborhood farm stands, community-supported agriculture (CSA) programs, and other initiatives that involve communities in their own food destinies. Strength To Love 2 is an amazing hidden pocket of sixteen hoop houses on two formerly vacant blocks in the Sandtown-Winchester neighborhood. The farm uses sustainable methods to grow produce for sale at local farmers markets, corner stores, and at Avenue Market, one of Baltimore's historic public markets, while providing job training for ex-offenders returning to society.

Another strategy has been to look at where the city can make independent changes to procurement. For instance, for all the talk about farm-to-school programs, the federal government's ludicrously low reimbursement for school lunch programs ($3.23 per meal, plus 6¢ extra if meals meet the new nutrition guidelines!) makes it close to impossible for a large school district to prioritize local, healthy, and sustainable sourcing. However, the city has been able to embed good food procurement principles in its summer youth meals program, where the funding streams are different and they have more flexibility in procurement.

In addition to the staff position for a food policy director, Baltimore's Food Policy Initiative includes a Food Policy Action Coalition, known as Food PAC, with members representing nonprofits, universities, farms, businesses, hospitals, and residents. In 2017, Freishtat and her team also piloted a special advisory panel of Resident Equity Advisors, residents of the communities served by the organizations involved with Food PAC, in an effort to be intentional about shifting power to community members, "so that I'm not the messenger coming to them, but we create a space for their voices."

Other policy changes have included: designation of Food Desert Retail Incentive Areas, to provide tax credits for the establishment of supermarkets; allowing residents to keep chickens, rabbits, bees, and even pygmy goats; and

Chesapeake Region Food Policy Councils

The Johns Hopkins University Center for a Livable Future's Food Policy Networks website (http://www.foodpolicynetworks.org/) hosts a database of food policy councils from across the country, among a plethora of other resources that support the development of effective state and local food policy through networking, capacity building, research, and technical assistance.

Adams County Food Policy Council (PA)
http://www.adamsfoodpolicy.org /index.html
> Envisions that all residents of Adams County will have access to a safe, nutritious, affordable, and adequate food supply within a sustainable system that promotes the local economy.

Arlington Urban Agriculture Task Force (VA)
http://home.arlingtonurbanag.org/home
> Arlington Friends of Urban Agriculture facilitates community collaboration to promote sustainable food systems for Arlington, Virginia.

Baltimore Food Policy Initiative (MD)
http://www.baltimoresustainability.org /projects/baltimore-food-policy-initiative /food-pac/
> Facilitated by the Baltimore Food Policy Initiative, Food Policy Action Coalition (Food PAC) provides opportunities for collaboration and idea sharing around food-related organizations in Baltimore. Members are invested in issues ranging from food policy, food justice, childhood hunger, food access, nutrition, obesity, food retail, and research in food systems.

Charlottesville Food Justice Network (VA)
https://www.cityschoolyardgarden.org/ programs/charlottesville-food-justice- network/
> A collaborative rather than a policy council, this organization fosters collaboration among local organizations working in unique and complementary ways to build a healthy and just community food system.

DC Food Policy Council
https://dcfoodpolicy.org/
> A coalition of stakeholders and government representatives who have come together to identify regulatory burdens on the local food economy, collect and analyze data on the food economy and food equity, promote positive food policies, and guide organizations and individuals involved in the food economy to promote food access, food sustainability, and a local food economy in the District.

Delaware Urban Farm and Food Coalition
https://www.thedch.org/what-we-do /community-gardens/urban-farm-coalition
> The mission of the Delaware Urban Farm and Food Coalition is to support community-oriented urban agricultural projects that expand healthy food access in northern Delaware and bring together resources and technical assistance through a collaborative approach to urban farming.

Fairfax Food Council (VA)
http://www.fairfaxcounty.gov/hd/fairfax -food-council/
> A coalition of citizens who advocate and promote food system and policy changes benefitting Fairfax communities, especially underserved communities.

Lehigh Valley Food Policy Council (PA)
https://www.facebook.com/LVFood PolicyCouncil/
> Strengthens the local food economy by increasing access to fresh food, reducing food insecurity and supporting Lehigh Valley farming.

Mid-Shore Food
System Coalition (MD)
http://fixourfood.info/
A strategic body that identifies, prioritizes, and coordinates food-system improvements in the five-county (Caroline, Dorchester, Kent, Queen Anne's, and Talbot) mid-Shore region, with an eye toward improving community resilience and triple-bottom-line sustainability.

Montgomery County Food Council (MD)
http://mocofoodcouncil.org/
An independent council formed and led by individual community members and representatives of local businesses, government, nonprofit organizations, and educational institutions, connecting all individuals and organizations committed to cultivating a robust, sustainable, and equitable food system in Montgomery County, Maryland.

Philadelphia Food Policy
Advisory Council (PA)
https://phillyfpac.org/
Connects Philadelphians and their local government to create a more just food system and envisions that all Philadelphians can access and afford healthy, sustainable, culturally appropriate, local, and fair (related to demographics, labor practices, sourcing, and other factors) food.

Prince George's County Food
Equity Council (MD)
http://pgcfec.org/
The Prince George's County Food Equity Council (FEC) will develop and support policies, approaches, procedures, practices, and initiatives to create systemic change to the local food system, promoting health, economic opportunity, food security, and well-being, especially among communities that have been negatively impacted by the current food system.

RVA Food Collaborative (VA)
http://rvafoodcollaborative.com/about/
A forum for communication, collaboration, and collective thought on food system issues in the Richmond region. It's a way of sharing information about work being done, communicating about project needs, finding ways to be stronger together, and thinking like a community.

Southern Maryland Food Council
http://www.somdfoodcouncil.com/
Brings together diverse stakeholders to integrate critical aspects of the regional food system in order to sustain and enhance the environmental, economic, social, and nutritional health and sustainability of Southern Maryland.

Virginia Food System Council
http://www.virginiafoodsystemcouncil.org
The Virginia Food System Council's mission is to work to advance a nutrient-rich and safe food system for Virginians at all income levels, with an emphasis on access to local food, successful linkages between food producers and consumers, and a healthy, viable future for Virginia's farmers and farmland.

Western Maryland Food Council
http://www.wmdfoodcouncil.com/
The mission of the Western Maryland Food Council is to bring together diverse stakeholders to integrate the aspects of the food system to sustain and enhance the environmental, economic, social, and nutritional health of Western Maryland.

West Virginia Food and Farm Coalition
http://wvfoodandfarm.org/
Develops regional foodsheds and builds connections among those foodsheds by increasing food and farm business, promoting access to local foods, sharing resources, changing agricultural policy, mapping and connecting the local food sector, and telling West Virginia's food and farm story.

The Prince George's County Food Equity Council gathered residents of all ages, food system stakeholders, and elected officials to discuss health disparities in the county at its first Food Equity Forum in 2015. Photo by Gul Guleryuz.

allowing city employees to use their health reimbursement accounts to pay for CSA subscriptions.

Other Food Policy Council Examples

Washington, DC's, Food Policy and Director Establishment Act of 2014 created a food policy council and the position of Food Policy Director. Made up of twelve members appointed from the community and ten DC agency heads, the DC Food Policy Council has been developing a citywide food assessment and has made grocery store access for all who live in the underserved neighborhoods east of the Potomac River its top priority for 2018.

In suburban Maryland, the Prince George's County Food Equity Council, formed in 2013, is independent of government but has been endorsed by the County Council and provided with standing opportunities to bring its findings and recommendations to county lawmakers. It has successfully lobbied to retain funding for key positions that support the county's agricultural development, as well as for the restoration of local funding to nutrition benefits programs at farmers markets. The Prince George's County Food Equity

Council has also engaged the community through public stakeholder discussions and local candidate forums on food issues.

In neighboring Montgomery County, Maryland, the Montgomery County Food Council has worked with the County Council on the development of the County's Food Security Plan and is working on a comprehensive Food Action Plan that will encompass food literacy, food economy, and food recovery and access. The group has compiled and published a number of resources, including the Montgomery County Food and Beverage Guide and the Montgomery County Food Assistance Resource Directory.

Other food policy councils are focused on specific topics, such as urban agriculture in Fairfax and Arlington, and many are still in the early stages of building their collaborative framework and determining priorities. And food policy councils are not limited to urban and suburban communities but address the unique food access and economic development issues of rural areas as well.

The Mid-Shore Food System Coalition, which comprises five Eastern Shore counties of Maryland that have only 3 percent of the state's population but 32 percent of its farmland, the majority of it in poultry and grain farming, acknowledges a changing view of the agricultural practices that have defined the region for decades:

> Recently . . . the region has been affected by an evolving understanding of the ecological linkages between farming practices and Chesapeake Bay watershed health; associated and rapidly evolving regulations; current practices and public health. In addition, community efforts to improve regional food security, hunger, and labor conditions for agricultural employees are driving changes in the regional conversation. Indicators of hunger and food insecurity in the region, coupled with indicators of diet-related disease and mortality, make plain the opportunity for improvements in the regional food system.

Other Food Policy Actors

Regional collaborations between states and counties, private funders, food producers, and multi-jurisdictional organizations can identify overlap and redundancies, as well as gaps and conflicts, created by the political boundaries within our regional foodshed. These groups catalyze conversations across county and state borders and bring outside resources to bear on issues that affect consumers and producers regardless of the jurisdiction.

One such group is known as Washington Regional Food Funders, a working group of foundations including Kaiser Permanente, Prince Charitable Trusts, Town Creek Foundation, and others working on issues related to food in local communities, including food access, food justice, sustainable agriculture, hunger, nutrition, and diet-related disease. Through a series of assessments and stakeholder meetings, the group created a strategic plan that identified the need for philanthropy in food systems work to apply a stronger "equity lens" to projects being funded. An equity lens is described as:

> a magnifying glass to identify avoidable, unnecessary or unintentional barriers, exclusions and lack of opportunities to achieving good wellbeing. It prompts a system which considers factors like gender, age, socioeconomic status, disability, language, culture, race, ethnicity, sexual orientation, religious beliefs and geography when planning, implementing and evaluating elements of the food system (not to exclude services or programs). It also encourages the system to consider the impact of discrimination, social cohesion, or isolation, levels of support, control over life choices; and includes the voices of those most affected by the barriers.

Money talks, and the weight of these funders has very quickly pushed equity to the forefront of many food systems conversations and made organizations that were otherwise acting in good faith more aware of the need to examine their own operations using an equity lens as well.

Other examples of groups working regionally to influence food policies include the Chesapeake Bay Foundation, which works across all six states in the Chesapeake Bay watershed, but primarily in Maryland, Virginia, and Pennsylvania, to teach farmers conservation and sustainable agriculture practices that reduce the negative impacts of agriculture on the Bay. They also advocate for effective laws and regulations to protect and improve the region's water quality in these states' legislatures and on the federal level. The Metropolitan Washington Council of Governments is currently pursuing an initiative to bring the DC area's local governments together around strengthening regional supply chain infrastructure, such as food hubs and local transportation networks, to bring greater volumes of locally grown and raised food to market. The Chesapeake Foodshed Network is building a framework

Veggies from Trucks and Horses

Getting food to neighborhoods that are underserved by the food system sometimes requires innovative solutions. Mobile farmers markets can reach more neighborhoods more efficiently than setting up individual farmers markets where demand may not support the sales needed to keep several farmers returning week after week.

The Arcadia Center for Sustainable Food and Agriculture, based in Alexandria, Virginia, converted a school bus to a farm-stand-on-wheels that makes more than a dozen stops across Washington, DC, and Northern Virginia during the growing season. Baltimore's Real Food Farm rolls out its van full of fresh veggies at eight or more locations throughout the city each week, including senior centers, community centers, and apartment complexes, for one- to two-hour windows. Real Food Farm will also make home deliveries. Before they could hit the streets with their local veggies, Civic Works, the nonprofit that operates Real Food Farm, had to work with the Baltimore city government to write new regula-

tions for mobile farmers markets, to avoid being subject to the same licensing requirements and fees as street food vendors.

But mobile markets are not as new an idea as they seem. Street vendors called Arabbers (pronounced "AY-rabbers") drove horse-drawn carts, hawking fresh fruits and vegetables through working-class neighborhoods in cities along the East Coast into the mid-twentieth century. Today, Baltimore is the only city to still have a few active Arabbers, many of whom come from families that have plied the streets with produce for generations. The tradition started with black men who couldn't find other work following the Civil War. Arabbers continued to provide a valuable community service to people in neighborhoods without grocery stores and to seniors unable to get around easily to shop. Baltimore's Arabber Preservation Society is working to preserve and improve the three public stables where Arabbers' horses are kept and to maintain this legacy of neighborhood self-sufficiency in the changing food landscape.

for connection, alignment, and collaborative action among the hundreds of organizations and individuals achieving great, but small, successes in their own silos, with the hope that a broader vision will catalyze deeper and more lasting change.

The task board for volunteer day at ECO City Farms. Photo by Sonia Keiner.

Building Community Helps Build Good Local Food Policy

These examples all show that conversations and collaborations across all parts of the food system can yield food systems change. It still feels like the gains are incremental, but as more of them pile up, they will clear a wider swath through the existing broken food system.

To keep it going, diverse consumers—affluent, low-income, and at points in between; urban, suburban, and rural residents; of African, European, Latino, Asian, Native American, and mixed heritage; omnivores, carnivores, pescatarians, vegetarians, vegans, and flexitarians; regardless of age, gender, marital status, skin color, or formal schooling—all need to be better educated about and empowered to make choices about the food we buy and eat.

We need more farmers working the land, operating many types of farms, of different sizes, growing a diversity of crops and livestock, and not just in rural areas. Those farmers need long-term access to land to establish their farms and invest the time and effort needed to nurture healthy soil. We need to make capital available to invest in entrepreneurial local farming and food production, and we need the political will to knock down barriers and build up bridges that allow farmers and farm businesses to exist and flourish.

We need to continue making space for conversations that let us talk about differences and also come together over shared meals. The more we foster the people-to-people interactions that have brought the local food movement this far, the better we'll be able to weave all the individual great work taking place all over our region into a coherent local food system, one that creates shared *value* and is driven by shared *values*.

Maple Pecan Pie

Traditional pecan pie gets its texture from the combination of corn syrup and sugar. Here I've used syrup and sugar, both from local maple sap. It makes for a slightly softer filling that has a depth of flavor, not just a wall of sweetness. When you use local whole-grain flour, the crust has flecks of nutty bran and a crumbly texture that is a perfect foil for the richness of the maple filling. But it can be temperamental to handle; a purchased pie crust works well, too.

2 cups whole-grain all-purpose flour
½ teaspoon coarse salt
1 teaspoon sugar
¾ cup unsalted butter, cold
3–4 tablespoons ice water
3 eggs
¾ cup pure maple syrup
¾ cup maple sugar
2 tablespoons melted butter
1¼ cups chopped pecans

For the crust: Stir together flour, salt, and sugar, then cut in butter using a pastry cutter or two knives until it forms clumps the size of small peas. Sprinkle ice water over the mixture and mix swiftly until the mass comes together in a ball. Divide into two halves. Pat each out into a disk on a large square of plastic wrap. Put one in the refrigerator for 30 minutes to 1 hour. Put the other in the freezer for future use.

Preheat the oven to 350°F.

After the dough has chilled, place it on a floured board and roll gently to a circumference to fit a 9-inch pie shell. Keep the surface well floured. When the dough is at the right size, carefully roll it up onto your rolling pin to transfer it to the pie plate. This dough will be prone to breaking, but just squeeze any little holes together with your fingers and patch large holes with pieces of broken dough. Place the pie plate on a cookie sheet.

In a large mixing bowl, beat the eggs slightly, then beat in the maple syrup, maple sugar, and melted butter. Add the pecans and stir to incorporate. Pour the filling into the crust, and move it around with a spoon a little to ensure the pecans are evenly distributed. Carefully place the cookie sheet on the middle rack of the oven. Bake for 45–50 minutes or until the pie puffs up like a dome and does not jiggle when you gently shake the pan. Remove from the oven. The puffiness will shrink as the pie cools. Serve slightly warm or chilled. Serves 8–10.

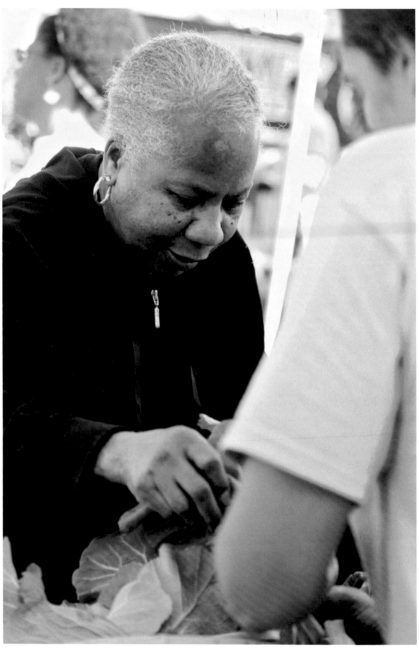

My mother, Geneva Brooks, enjoys buying collards at the Riverdale Park Farmers Market. Photo by Sonia Keiner

8 | Make Your Choices Count

I originally planned to end this book with a chapter recreating the local food experiment recounted in the article from *Mother Earth News* in the introduction. I thought it might be a good way to demonstrate how much shopping for local food has changed in the last decade. I wanted to leave you with the confidence that it is not as hard as it used to be or as hard as you might think to eat local, just in case everything you've read to this point hasn't convinced you.

My life has changed quite a bit since Kristi and I wrote that article in 2006. Then, I was a freelance writer, working from home, with two small children who spent their days at the elementary school two blocks away. I made finding and cooking local food my part-time job, which eventually led to more writing, publishing, and nonprofit work related to local sustainable food. In a way, I was part of the elite at the time, because although I did not have a lot of disposable income, I did have the time to research and run down the food sources I wanted, the skill to cook from scratch, and the familiarity with a range of different ingredients through my family background and experiences living abroad.

Today, I still have my food and cooking background, and I retain the accumulated knowledge of food sources in the area, but I now work a full-time job unrelated to food. Thankfully, my job is located close to home and allows me to work remotely as much as I like, so I still have the flexibility to spend time sourcing and cooking local food, but not as much as before. My kids are now in college. They are more independent in some ways but require more of my time in other ways as they navigate their transitions to adulthood. They also eat more, when they eat at home. Deciding to start this book during my daughter's first year of college and finishing it as my son gets ready to start his first year was not the least stressful timing I could have chosen.

But through the process of putting this book together and experimenting with as many ways of sourcing local food as I could manage, I have realized that my way of eating local now is so different than it was ten or twelve years ago that a one-month chronicle would seem more of a gimmick than a helpful roadmap. When there were very few avenues to take and the internet was an information country road rather than a superhighway in comparison with what's available online today, the local food experiment was an instructive way to help others get started without having to exert as much effort as we did.

This book is stuffed with resources about local food, and there is so much more to be found online and in your own community. There is no one way to "eat local" because all of our lives are different, our personal resources of money, time, transportation, interest, tastes, and food skills are different. The way I engage with local food changes given my resources and stresses at any given moment. But I have put together a selection of recommended "First Steps" following this chapter that might help you figure out a good place to start.

Despite all the information here, there is so much that I couldn't include and that I don't know myself. I imagine you still have questions that you wish had been answered here but were not. That's not necessarily a bad thing. I expect to continue learning new things about the local food system as long as I continue eating. I hope your lingering questions will spur you to seek out answers and to start or deepen your engagement with the local food system.

Don't be the person who complains when the neighborhood farmers market or locally sourced restaurant closes but who never shopped there because the prices were a bit higher than the chain store or restaurant. Spending just $5 or $10 at the local shop on a regular basis can make a huge difference, especially if everyone who thinks of it does it.

How many people told me they wished they had subscribed to or placed an ad in *Edible Chesapeake* when they found out I had to close it? Let the farmers and shopkeepers and restaurateurs you patronize know where you heard about them and encourage them to advertise and support the media that inform you.

If you have the financial means to help others, make an ongoing monthly contribution to support a community garden, a food education program in schools, or the matching dollars program at a farmers market that serves a low-income population.

Pay attention, no matter where you shop, and look for opportunities to support local sourcing. If people don't buy the locally grown salad mixes at Giant or the local tomatoes at Whole Foods, the grocery buyers will say, "See? No one wanted the local produce." They'll stop stocking it, we'll lose that choice, and a local company with the scale to supply large quantities of produce could face failure. Don't let that happen.

Keep an open mind about the ways we can produce good food closer to the people who will eat it, and keep in mind that the status quo probably wasn't so at some point in the past. People in most cities used to have the ability to keep a couple of chickens, giving families of limited financial means a nutritious protein source. Likewise, moving to an outer suburb or rural area for the country atmosphere means keeping an open mind about the ways to keep that rural land in active agricultural production.

When people say they don't think their one vote counts, then are disappointed that the election doesn't go their way, it's too late to go back and do what they should have done in the first place. It's the same with our agricultural resources, especially in a rapidly developing area like our Chesapeake region. Every choice you make affects what's on your plate and mine. Let's all make our choices count.

First Steps

I keep making the point that there are endless ways to eat local, but every journey of a thousand miles must begin with one step. This list breaks down the options to identify a few suggestions of where to begin your local eating journey, depending on what kind of shopper-cook-eater you are. You can flip back through the pages of the book to find the directories that will help you try just one of these activities as a first step. That's all it takes to get started, and everyone who takes one step adds a little more strength to the local food system.

If you qualify for federal food assistance:

* *Use SNAP (Supplemental Nutrition Assistance Program), WIC, and Senior checks at the farmers market.* Farmers markets across the region, especially those serving low-income and food-insecure communities, accept these programs for fresh produce purchases. WIC or Senior Farmers Market Nutrition Program checks are an incentive that can only be used at farmers markets, so don't leave this benefit on the table if you are an eligible WIC recipient.

* *Get extra dollars at the farmers market.* Farmers markets that accept benefits can often help add to your purchasing power through matching programs that give you additional money to spend. For instance, in DC, the Produce Plus Program provides $10 a week to spend on farmers market produce to anyone who receives a wide range of federal food, disability, or income assistance benefits. Maryland Market Money and Virginia Fresh Match also offer matching dollars.

* *Join a work-share CSA (community-supported agriculture).* If you have an interest in growing and two to four hours a week to volunteer on

the farm, you can earn a free CSA share with farms such as Clagett Farm and Owl's Nest Farm, both in Upper Marlboro, Maryland, or Three Part Harmony Farm and Common Good City Farm in DC. Some farms also offer income-qualified sliding-scale payments for CSA shares.

If you want to test out the local food waters without spending much:

* *Join a CSA with sliding-scale payments.* Some CSAs let members pay what they can afford on a sliding scale. Members who can pay more help make up the difference for those who pay less. Seven Springs Farm in Floyd, Virginia, is an example, with a range of prices for shares of different sizes.

* *Eat rescued produce.* A lot of the produce rescued by Hungry Harvest comes from local farms, especially in the summer, and would otherwise be trashed or composted. A mini-harvest box is only $15 and contains about eight items, such as hydroponic lettuce, vine-ripened or heirloom tomatoes, apples, Asian pears, zucchini, potatoes, and more.

* *Make just one farmers market purchase each week.* Go to your local farmers market with just $10 in your pocket. That's how much the Maryland Buy Local Challenge and the Virginia Eat Local Challenge say would make a difference, if everyone in the state took part. Buy a couple of quarts of strawberries or blueberries for a shortcake at the height of the season. Bring a huge watermelon to your extended family's July 4th cookout. Splurge on a pound of luxurious pastured bacon for a special breakfast.

If shopping is not your priority, have local food delivered:

* *Subscribe to a home delivery CSA.* Check around your neighborhood to see who subscribes to a CSA that delivers. Usually there need to be a certain number of people in the area to make it economically feasible for the farmer to deliver to individual homes or a central neighborhood pick-up spot.

* *Order a box from a food hub delivery program.* 4P Foods, Washington's Green Grocer, From the Farmer, Hometown Harvest, and other delivery services offer local-only produce bags starting at around

$35 for a small share that will keep two people in veggies and fruit for a week. You can also order local meat, dairy, and egg shares, as well as additional items a la carte.

* *Have soup delivered*. Soupergirl will deliver delicious, plant-based soups made from scratch, with local ingredients identified on each label, directly to your home. You can either order online by the Tuesday deadline for delivery on Wednesday or Thursday, or set up a "soupscription" and have your weekly allowance of soups delivered like clockwork.

If you want someone else to cook:

* *Eat at the farmers market*. Farmers markets such as the FRESH-FARM Market at Dupont Circle and others have plenty to offer for those who prefer their local bounty ready to eat. Maybe you'll be lucky enough to go on a day when Bev Eggleston of EcoFriendly Foods is dishing up "the South in your mouth"—shaved country ham, yellow coarse-ground grits, kale, and okra cooked down southern style, all topped with a farm-fresh poached egg, every ingredient from his Virginia farm.

* *Grab a quick local lunch*. A $10 salad bowl at one of Sweetgreens' twenty-three locations in greater DC and Baltimore is likely to have at least one seasonal veggie or locally made cheese in it. Atwater's six Baltimore locations may have tomatoes from their own farm along with other local ingredients. Slurp down a few Virginia bivalves at the Rappahannock Oyster Company's raw bar at Union Market in DC, grab a Virginia grass-fed beef burger at any Busboys and Poets, or sink your teeth into a Virginia flat-iron steak topped with Maryland's FireFly Farms' blue cheese for under $20 at Silver Diner locations throughout the area.

* *Find chefs who care*. Monica Alvarado of Bread and Butter Kitchen in Annapolis started out at the Anne Arundel County Farmers Market, alongside many of her suppliers. Cunningham's in Towson, Maryland, sources from its own Cunningham Farms in nearby Baltimore County. The Restaurant at Patowmack Farm in Lovettsville, Virginia, overlooking the Potomac River, is actually on the farm. The farmers of the Chesapeake Farm to Table food hub list on their website the

thirty or so Baltimore-area caterers, purveyors, and restaurants that feature their local products. If a restaurant's menu and staff leave you unsure about the food, check for a local beer, wine, or cocktail.

If you are a weekly shopper:

* *Pick a farmers market to visit regularly.* Choose the most convenient location, which could be near your home on the weekend or near your office on a weekday evening. Pack your reusable bags and hit the market with a mind open to the possibilities presented by what's for sale that day. You can pay with credit cards at many markets or individual farmers stands, but carrying cash may help you control how much you spend.

* *Shop for some of your everyday items at a store that sources locally.* Get familiar with what they carry and decide what local products you can commit to. Maybe you'll switch to local eggs from pasture-raised hens and local milk from grass-fed cows instead of the supermarket brands. It might be manageable to buy a pound of local grass-fed ground beef once or twice a month, even if you don't buy all your meat from local sources.

* *Join a CSA that offers on-farm pick-up.* Some CSAs are set up to allow you to pack your own share, with guidelines about how much of each item you can take. It's like going to the store to shop for vegetables, except the store is a farm and you don't have to pay every time you go.

If you have room for food storage:

* *Buy meat in bulk.* If you have freezer space, buy meat in bulk and save dollars per pound. For example, a split quarter of local grass-fed beef can range from about 80 to 120 pounds and cost around $7-$10 per pound, which means you are paying about the cost of ground beef for an assortment of ground, stew meat, roasts, and steaks. Grain-finished local beef can cost a little less per pound. Find two or three others and buy a split quarter together if you want to control costs.

* *Join a CSA.* I know I've recommended a CSA for almost every kind of local eater, but that's because there is a CSA that will work for

almost everyone. Go for a large share if you are comfortable cooking, freezing, canning, and otherwise wrangling produce.

* *Pick your own produce.* Spending a few hours at a pick-your-own farm can be a fun and relatively economical way to get large quantities of strawberries, blueberries, apples, peaches, and other fruit. It's a great option if you are prepared to cook, can, and freeze your picked bounty right away while it's at the peak of freshness.

If you're just curious:

* *Shop at a farm stand or farm store.* Roadside produce stands are often on the edge of the farm, giving you a glimpse of the fields or orchards under production. I've driven past pecking chickens and turkeys, grazing sheep and goats, even bison standing in the fields on my way to farm stores to buy local meat. At South Mountain Creamery in Middletown, Maryland, you can watch the dairy cows go through the milking parlor while enjoying your ice cream.

* *Attend a farm dinner or festival.* Farms on their own or in conjunction with restaurant or catering chefs often host dinners in their barns or fields. Equinox Restaurant held an "outstanding on the roof" dinner with Rooftop Acres in DC. These dinners can range from folksy to fancy, but they are always delicious. Lots of craft, art, music, and even fairy festivals are held at farms, vineyards, and breweries.

* *Enjoy some farm fun.* Many farms generate additional revenue through agri-tourism activities such as corn mazes, petting zoos, pumpkin patches, and hayrides. These farms are great places for school field trips and for kids' birthday parties.

* *Volunteer.* There are urban farms and orchard projects, food forests, and therapeutic farms across our area that rely on volunteers to help with all aspects of farm work. You can also get a great farm experience by volunteering with a network that gleans produce left in fields after the main harvest for donation to local food banks.

Acknowledgments

F irst thanks go to John Shields, a great friend and local food hero, for encouraging me when I first pitched this idea and for introducing me to the great folks at Johns Hopkins University Press. I'm very grateful to Catherine Goldstead at JHU Press, who saw the potential in my ramblings and helped me solidify a form and structure to contain them, as well as the entire publishing team that brought this project from dream to reality. I'd also like to thank writing coach Gina Hagler, who provided a few well-placed pieces of organizational advice that helped this first-time book author bring clarity and coherence to a mass of information.

I am a first-time author, but not a full-time author. The members of the Potomac Valley Chapter of the American Institute of Architects, whom I have the privilege of serving as executive director, have been incredibly supportive of my work on this book for the past two years. I also must thank my colleague Pam Rich, who generously covered the bases during my writing breaks.

The romantic notion of drafting a book on the kitchen table in snatches of time before work and between meals and family activities only gets you so far in real life before the need for a room of one's own becomes critical. Thank you, Jon Labovitz and Susanna Battin, for the extended period of writing at West Virginia's North Mountain Residency. It was a needed boost to my productivity and my confidence. I'm also very grateful to my old friend Mary Grace McGeehan and my new friend Patti Miller, who each gave me a room with a view and a fireplace in their West Virginia retreats when I needed a few days of writing focus.

I thank the many farmers and food systems friends I've come to know while publishing *Edible Chesapeake* and during my years of affiliation with ECO City Farms, the Riverdale Park Farmers Market, FRESHFARM Markets, Future Harvest–CASA, and, more recently, the Chesapeake Foodshed

Network. Their expertise and experiences have informed not only this book, but my own relationship with food. They are idealists and visionaries, as well as gritty fighters committed to driving positive change, in the face of systemic obstacles only slightly less daunting than the obstacles nature throws in the way of growing great food.

Kristi Bahrenburg Janzen has been my partner in local food exploration and writing from the beginning. She inspires me through her achievements as a local food and farming advocate, as a journalist and editor, and as a writer of both fiction and nonfiction. She has encouraged me to "lean in" to my own potential, when I haven't been so sure of it myself. Thank you, my friend.

My love of great food is rooted in my love for my family, where great food is always on the table. Thanks to my sister, Stacy Brooks, and my brother, Vincent Brooks III, both excellent and creative cooks, as well as great sounding boards for discussions of various food trends and ingredients. Stacy is always ready to attend a festival or local shop somewhere off the beaten path with me, and she also happens to be a great editor. She helped me immensely by reading parts of the manuscript, while on maternity leave, no less.

My mom, Geneva Brooks, is always the most vocal cheerleader in my corner, and has an unbounded faith in my ability to do whatever I say I'm going to do, no matter how pie-in-the-sky it sounds. My late father, Vincent Brooks, was more taciturn but no less stalwart in his support and willingness to help. My parents never trumpeted the sacrifices they made to see me and my siblings follow our dreams, but those sacrifices are nevertheless known, appreciated and, I hope, justified by what we've done with the opportunities.

Finally, I have to thank my amazing husband, Damon, and our fantastic children, Catie and Louis, who have put on a good game face during these two years while I've been writing about food more than cooking it. Eating local has been an adventure we've shared as a family from the start, and it will always be a defining part of our lives. I love them all so much and, in both my family and Damon's, cooking for each other and enjoying each other's cooking are among the ways that we show that love.

Recommended Reading

T hese are books that I have found useful, some as background for this book, all as good references on food and drink in the Chesapeake region.

Beyond Jefferson's Vines: The Evolution of Quality Wine in Virginia
by Richard G. Leahy
> Leahy explores the roots and growth of the Virginia wine industry, along with an insider's tour of Virginia's distinct wine regions.

Chesapeake Bay Cooking with John Shields, Twenty-Fifth Anniversary Edition
by John Shields. Photographs but Jed Kirschbaum
> Published in 2015, this book updates Shields' companion cookbook to his PBS series of the same name with a new chapter on the region's libations, primarily of the alcoholic kind, more online resources, and plenty of the down-to-earth Baltimore wit Shields is known for.

Dishing Up Maryland: 150 Recipes from the Alleghenies to the Chesapeake Bay
by Lucie L. Snodgrass. Foreword by John Shields. Photography by Edwin Remsberg
> Celebrate the state's signature flavors with recipes gathered from farmers and watermen, season by season.

Dishing Up Virginia: 145 Recipes That Celebrate Colonial Traditions and Contemporary Flavors by Patrick Evans-Hylton. Foreword by Marcel Desaulniers. Photography by Edwin Remsberg
> Learn about the history and innovation of Virginia cooking through recipes that celebrate the state's unique culinary regions.

Eat Local For Less: The Ultimate Guide to Opting Out of Our Broken Industrial Food System by Julie Castillo
> Castillo is a Maryland-based writer and anthropology professor who shares her experience in this primer on shifting to a local eating lifestyle, with asides on the cultural history of food and eating.

Edible Blue Ridge, Edible DC, and *Edible Delmarva*
> The quarterly *Edible* magazines (Baltimore should be joining soon) keep you up to date on local food trends and events, farms, producers, and restaurants.

Gaining Ground: A Story of Farmers' Markets, Local Food, and Saving the Family Farm by Forrest Pritchard
> This memoir from Forrest Pritchard of Smith Meadows Farm in Purcellville, Virginia, tells his story of coming back to a family farm on the verge of collapse in the 1990s and building it into a mainstay of the most successful farmers markets in the region. Gently humorous throughout, there are many laugh-out-loud moments that illustrate the challenges of selling food to local consumers.

Maryland Wine: A Full-Bodied History by Regina McCarthy
> This slim volume recounts the history of the Maryland wine industry, brings to life local wine pioneers who influenced wine-making across the country, and explains how the industry organized and created a legislative approach that has opened the way for the growth that continues today.

My Organic Life: How a Pioneering Chef Helped Shape the Way We Eat Today by Nora Pouillon
> In this enlightening memoir, chef and restaurateur Nora Pouillon shares the story of her quest to open the city's eyes to the farm bounty just outside its borders, launching the region's local food movement.

The New Chesapeake Kitchen by John Shields. Photographs by David W. Harp
> Published in 2018, this wonderful cookbook celebrates Chesapeake "Bay- and body-friendly" food. From crab dishes to seasonal soups, from local meats to fresh veggies and fruits, from canning to pickling, Shields includes it all, even some of his "secret" signature recipes.

Reclaiming Our Food: How the Grassroots Food Movement Is Changing the Way We Eat by Tanya Denckla Cobb. Foreword by Gary Paul Nabhan. Photo essays by Jason Houston
> All of the case studies in this survey of local food initiatives around the country are interesting and inspiring, and it includes several examples of work being done in the mid-Atlantic as well.

Seafood Lover's Chesapeake Bay: Restaurants, Markets, Recipes & Traditions by Mary Lou Baker with Holly Smith
> A compact survey of places to savor Chesapeake Bay seafood in Maryland along the Upper Bay, Eastern Shore, Western Shore and Southern Maryland, with entertaining lore and back stories.

The Wild Vine: A Forgotten Grape and the Untold Story of American Wine by Todd Kliman
> This book is a deep dive into the Virginia wine world via the Norton grape, a native variety that oenophiles either love or hate, and its most ardent promoter, Jenni McCloud of Chrysalis Vineyards.

Bibliography

Allen, Standish K., Jr. *Virginia's Spawnless Oyster: Traditionally Bred, Not Genetically Modified.* Gloucester Point, VA: Virginia Institute of Marine Science.

Badger, Curtis. *Clams: How to Find, Catch, and Cook Them.* Mechanicsburg, PA: Stackpole Books, 2002.

Ball Blue Book of Preserving. Muncie, IN: Jarden Home Brands, 2005.

Bowens, Natasha. *The Color of Food: Stories of Race, Resilience and Farming.* Gabriola Island, Canada: New Society Publishers, 2015.

Carman, Tim. "Rice Grown in Maryland? Farmer Sees a Future That Doesn't Involve Flooding." *Washington Post*, December 17, 2013.

Chesapeake Bay Maritime Museum. *Chesapeake Bay Maritime Museum.* Virginia Beach: Donning Company Publishers, 2003.

DeVaughn, David. *Case Study: Baltimore Food Policy Initiative.* Sustainable Cities Institute at the National League of Cities. 2012. http://www.sustainablecitiesinstitute .org/Documents/SCI/Case_Study/Baltimore_FoodPolicyInitiative_2013.pdf.

Ellsworth, Jessica. The History of Organic Food Regulation. 2001. https://dash.harvard .edu/handle/1/8889458.

Fallon, Sally, and Mary Enig. *Nourishing Traditions.* Revised 2nd ed. Washington, DC: NewTrends, 2001.

Ficara, John Francis, and Juan Williams. *Black Farmers in America.* Lexington: University Press of Kentucky, 2006.

Future Harvest–Chesapeake Alliance for Sustainable Agriculture and Maryland Grazers Network. *Amazing Grazing Directory.* 2016. https://www.futureharvestcasa .org/resources/amazing-grazing-directory-0.

Halweil, Brian. *Eat Here: Reclaiming Homegrown Pleasures in a Global Supermarket.* New York: W. W. Norton, 2004.

Janzen, Kristi Bahrenburg. "Loss of Small Slaughterhouses Hurts Farmers, Butchers and Consumers." *Farming Magazine,* Winter 2004.

Kennedy, Rhea Yablon. "How Researchers Are Trying to Grow an Unusual Urban Crop: Rice." *Washington Post*, September 10, 2015.

Leahy, Richard. *Beyond Jefferson's Vines: The Evolution of Quality Wine in Virginia*. New York: Sterling Epicure, 2012.

Madrecki, Thomas. How Sustainable Is Virginia Wine? *Edible DC,* Summer 2016.

McCarthy, Regina. *Maryland Wine: A Full-Bodied History*. Charleston, SC: History Press, 2012.

Planck, Nina. *Real Food: What to Eat and Why*. New York: Bloomsbury, 2006.

Pollan, Michael. *The Omnivore's Dilemma*. New York: Penguin Random House, 2006.

Pritchard, Forrest. *Gaining Ground: A Story of Farmers' Markets, Local Food, and Saving the Family Farm*. Guilford, CT: Lyons Press, 2013.

Shields, John. *The Chesapeake Bay Cookbook: Rediscovering the Pleasures of a Great Regional Cuisine*. Reading, MA: Aris Books, 1990.

Shields, John. *Chesapeake Bay Cooking with John Shields*. 25th anniversary edition. Baltimore: Johns Hopkins University Press, 2015.

Sussman, Lily, and Karen Bassarab. *Food Policy Council Report 2016*. Johns Hopkins Center for a Livable Future. 2016. https://assets.jhsph.edu/clf/mod_clfResource/doc/FPC%20Report%202016_Final.pdf.

Warner, William W. *Beautiful Swimmers: Watermen, Crabs and the Chesapeake Bay*. Boston: Back Bay Books / Little, Brown, 1976.

Watson, Lyall. *The Whole Hog: Exploring the Extraordinary Potential of Pigs*. Washington, DC: Smithsonian Books, 2004.

Winne, Mark, and Michael Burgan. *Doing Food Policy Councils Right: A Guide to Development and Action*. Mark Winne Associates. 2012. https://www.markwinne.com/wp-content/uploads/2012/09/FPC-manual.pdf.

Index